SOUTH CAROLINA'S HISTORIC RESTAURANTS

and their recipes

SOUTH
CAROLINA'S

JOHN F. BLAIR, *Publisher*
Winston-Salem, North Carolina

HISTORIC RESTAURANTS

and their recipes

by DAWN O'BRIEN
and KAREN MULFORD

Drawings by Bob Anderson, Patsy Faires and Debbie Hampton

1984 by DAWN O'BRIEN and KAREN MULFORD

Printed in the United States of America
Revised edition 1992
Book design by Virginia Ingram
Drawings by Bob Anderson, Patsy Faires and Debbie Hampton
Cover photographs by Bernard Carpenter
Composition by The Roberts Group
Manufactured by R. R. Donnelley & Sons

Library of Congress Cataloging in Publication Data

O'Brien, Dawn.
South Carolina's historic restaurants and their recipes.

Includes index.
1. Cookery, American—Southern style.   2. Cookery—
South Carolina.   3. Restaurants, lunch rooms, etc.—
South Carolina.   4. Historic buildings—South Carolina.
I. Mulford, Karen.   II. Title.
TX715.0'287   1984   641.5'09757   84-18556
ISBN 0-89587-097-5

DEDICATION

I believe the most important gift a child can receive is a sense of self-worth. Both of my late grandmothers, Etta Lee and Goldie West, knew how to inspire this feeling. Therefore, even though neither is alive to see how their gift is manifesting itself, I dedicate this book to them.

Dawn O'Brien

I'd like to thank my husband, Jon, and my sons, Sean and Justin, for their remarkable patience during the months of travel, research and writing involved in this book. Special thanks go to my parents, Bill and Leona Surina, for their encouraging support of this project—and all the others I've undertaken during my life.

Karen Mulford

ACKNOWLEDGMENTS

A project of this scope is a collaborative labor involving more people than just the writers. For those individuals and agencies who gave us help through endorsement, encouragement or the sharing of special skills, we are thankful.

To: The chefs who shared their secrets with us—especially those who, due to language barriers, took us back to their kitchens and taught us, step-by-step, their unique methods of preparation.

To: The restaurateurs who helped us discover the rich heritage of their establishments.

To: South Carolina's Division of Tourism, especially Director Robert G. Liming, travel writer Waltene G. Vaughn, Alice T. Hite, Joanna Angle, Jayne T. Redman, Diane Raef and Kevin Crown.

To: The many branches of South Carolina's Chamber of Commerce that provided material and assistance.

To: Betty Jo Gilley, Leona Surina, Irma and Bill Joyce and Barbara and Walter Pitts, who helped us test and retest recipes in the areas of their culinary expertise.

To: John, Shannon Heather and Daintry O'Brien for their continuing patience and interest in developing more sophisticated palates.

To: All our guinea pigs who ate the testing dishes, particularly those who gave us confidence when they asked for second helpings.

FOREWORD

From a contemporary sage comes this wisdom: "You can never be too rich or too thin." Neither condition has ever plagued me. But after feasting my way through a few hundred historic restaurants from Pennsylvania to Florida, it has become clear that, travel- and time-wise, I *could* spread myself too thin. It has grown more and more obvious just how much I need collaborators to share the "oh so tough" grind of dining lavishly. When Karen Mulford and I first met years ago, we clicked instantly. Maybe it's because we are both transplanted Westerners; I can't explain it. But in spite of living for many years below the Mason-Dixon line, neither of us has lost our appreciation for things Southern.

Even with such instant rapport, we privately wondered if one of us would end up killing the other. (Harsher thoughts have occurred to collaborators.) Instead, it has been a very positive experience. Among many lessons, we have discovered that frustrations are more bearable when they are shared.

On occasion, enthusiasm has gotten the better of us. While researching the revised edition of this book, it was particularly fun for me to see Karen race into Bocci's Italian Restaurant to meet me one noon. We had decided earlier that day to divide the appointments, and she could have gone to our inn and taken a nap, but the excitement this restaurant promised was too much of a temptation for her to miss.

Throughout our joint and separate travels, we have found that a specific question continually surfaces: "Is this building historic, or is it just old?" The answer lies in the definition of history and is one that is argued with unresolved scholarly pursuit.

Some historians believe a structure should be considered historic only if a significant national or regional event has occurred there. This view, in our opinion, denies the contributions of many of our nation's people. We feel that everyday people played a major role in the formation of our country's values. True, famed statesmen contributed to our lawmaking process, and their names are recorded in our textbooks, as they should be. Unrecorded, though, are those who helped to build our country through their simple daily toil. We think they count equally. Therefore, we have chosen not to ignore a beautiful old church, warehouse or post office simply because it was not the site of an event significant enough to be included in our history books.

Age is, of course, a basic factor in the formulation of historical criteria. Any structure less than fifty years old does not qualify for inclusion in this book. In researching the historic structures that have been transformed into restaurants in South Carolina, we have conformed to this requirement, with one exception: Rice Planters Restaurant in Myrtle Beach. This building was constructed from materials over one hundred years old, and we feel this tie to the past makes the restaurant a worthy candidate. After all, one of the criteria we value most is the preservation of materials that otherwise would have been destroyed.

We believe dining should be an event, not just a habit. In essence, this means that the atmosphere must equal the food. Thus, just as in the other six volumes in this series, not every historic restaurant in the state is included in this book. Within the framework of our criteria, which is as subjective as it is objective, not all the historic restaurants we visited met the standards that contribute to an enjoyable dining experience. Also, there are a few restaurants that are not included because they were not interested in participating or did not want to share their histories or recipes with us.

Incidentally, we feel it is important for readers to know that every recipe has been tested, and in some instances modified, for home use. My daughter Heather, now a recipe-testing veteran and a college senior, is often asked which dish is her favorite. Recently, I overheard her answer: "Which category? If we're talking entrées, it was that Reuben Chicken at Farmers Hall, which is a great dish you can make in a hurry. But with dessert, it would have to be that Banana Buttermilk Custard at Magnolias." My husband, John, interrupted any further recitations with, "What about Newton House's Taco Quiche, or that Vienna Cream Roll from Seven Oaks?" This enthusiasm should encourage readers to try even the seemingly difficult recipes. Believe me, it's not impossible to achieve fabulous results in your own kitchen.

Karen relates that her husband, Jon, favored the seafood dishes, while pasta recipes like Olive Oil's Pasta Rosé won raves from sons Sean and Justin. Today, all three Mulford men are quite comfortable in the family's recipe-testing kitchen, and each has become an enthusiastic cook. One dish that has earned "favorite standby" status in the Mulford kitchen is Villa Tronco Ristorante's Shrimp Fettuccine, a choice our food editor, Sue Clark, seconds. This is one of the perks of being a food editor; you get the second shot at trying out what makes you hungry.

From the experiences and feedback we have encountered in testing and serving these recipes, it can only be said that feasts await you, whether in South Carolina's historic restaurants or in your own kitchen. *Bon appétit!*

CONTENTS

Spartanburg

Greenville●

Clemson● ●Pendleton

●Anderson ●Laurens Winnsboro

●Abbeville Columbia

Aiken

Bennettsville●

●Camden

Florence

Little River

Myrtle Beach

Murrells Inlet

Summerville●

Mount Pleasant

Charleston

Beaufort

THE PARSON'S TABLE RESTAURANT
Little River

THE PARSON'S TABLE

Did you ever buy a clothing accessory so fantastic that you assembled an entire outfit around it? Then you will understand what longtime Little River resident Toby Frye did. He rescued some magnificent, opalescent stained-glass windows, which meant that he needed to find an equally magnificent location for their display. Since the stained glass was salvaged from churches, what could have been more suitable than Little River Methodist Church?

The church deserved some sprucing up. Since the Little River area was poor at the time the church was constructed in 1885, the building had no stained-glass windows to call its own until it was transformed into a restaurant. In 1978, the weathered-pine structure was moved to its present location. Then began the business of designing one of the most sophisticated interiors you'll ever see. Until you read the sign above the entrance, you may think you've stumbled upon a meticulously kept old church. The picket fence and gazebo suggest an earlier period, a time when this part of the beach area was a little sailing village.

But the view is quite different once you enter the restaurant. The interior of The Parson's Table reminded me a bit of Maxwell Plum's in New York. Some of the stained glass is lighted from the back and used to artistically partition the dining room and the kitchen. In one room, the stained glass forms the ceiling. There are other interesting touches as well. The hostess stand is actually an 1800 church pulpit held together entirely by wooden pegs, rather than nails. And the large chandelier near the entrance was originally a part of a Baptist church in Mullins.

In fact, the jeweled splendor of the glass and the numerous historical touches render such a magnificent effect that you wonder if the cuisine will be anticlimactic. It is not. Current owners Ed and Nancy Murray have a list of credentials thirty years long. Ed is a member of the prestigious, Paris-based Chaîne des Rôtisseurs, the world's oldest gastronomical society. Since the Murrays took over in 1988, The Parson's Table has been the recipient of many awards, ranging from the Silver Spoon to the International Award of Excellence to the Five

2

Diamond Award, which recognizes the top fifty overall restaurants in the United States.

My dinner was so scrumptiously orchestrated that I wondered how I would ever be able to duplicate it in my own kitchen. But thanks to management's encouragement, my recipe-testing fears proved groundless. For my entrée, I selected the indescribably good Lobster Thermidor. Dessert forced me to make another difficult choice. Their Amaretto Cheesecake with Barclay Sauce is the kind of mirage I'd see if stranded in the desert. It's so rich that a sliver is all you can manage, but it's a recipe that will make you famous. That's exactly what the Murrays have done for this stunning restaurant.

The Parson's Table Restaurant is located six miles north of North Myrtle Beach in Little River off U.S. 17. The restaurant is open from the Tuesday before Valentine's Day until the Saturday after Thanksgiving. Dinner is served from 5:00 p.m. until 9:30 p.m., Monday through Saturday. For reservations, call (803) 249-3702.

THE PARSON'S TABLE RESTAURANT'S
LOBSTER THERMIDOR

2 6-ounce lobster tails	1 teaspoon Dijon mustard
1 cup heavy cream	finely chopped parsley
3 teaspoons sherry	2 slices Gruyère or other
1 tablespoon Parmesan	white cheese
cheese	

Split lobster tails lengthwise across top of shell. Remove meat and dice into bite-size chunks. Place cream in saucepan and heat on medium-high. Add sherry and mustard and reduce heat until sauce starts to thicken. Add lobster meat and cook in sauce until meat is barely done. Remove meat and stuff back in shell. Top with sauce, Parmesan cheese, parsley and Gruyère cheese. Bake in 350-degree oven for 10 minutes or until the cheese melts. Place on heated platter and top with excess sauce. Serves 2.

THE PARSON'S TABLE RESTAURANT'S
AMARETTO CHEESECAKE WITH BARCLAY SAUCE

Amaretto Cheesecake:

1 graham-cracker crust (see Index)	**½ cup whipping cream**
2½ pounds cream cheese	**1 teaspoon salt**
1½ cups sugar	**1 tablespoon almond extract**
1 packet unflavored gelatin	**3 ounces amaretto**
	5 eggs

Prepare graham-cracker crust. Press it into a greased 10-inch springform pan and bake for 8 to 10 minutes at 350 degrees. Allow cream cheese to reach room temperature; cut into chunks. With an electric mixer, combine cream cheese with sugar and blend for 15 to 20 minutes. Dissolve gelatin in whipping cream over low heat, whisking constantly. Add to cream cheese mixture when gelatin is dissolved. Add remaining ingredients and mix on low speed until well combined. Pour batter into the crust. Set the springform pan into a large roasting pan placed on oven rack. Pour water around the springform pan, being careful not to spill any water into batter. Water should cover ⅔ the height of the cake pan. Bake at 300 degrees for about 2 hours, or until a toothpick comes out clean when inserted into cake. Let cake cool, then refrigerate several hours.

Barclay Sauce:

1 10-ounce package frozen strawberries or raspberries (or 5 ounces of each)	**1 cup crème de cassis or dry white wine**
1 10-ounce jar strawberry preserves	**1 shaved square of unsweetened chocolate**

Place berries, preserves and crème de cassis in a blender and purée until smooth. Cut Amaretto Cheesecake and pour sauce over each slice. Garnish with shaved chocolate. Yields 1 cake.

RICE PLANTERS RESTAURANT
Myrtle Beach

RICE PLANTERS RESTAURANT

There's not a doubt in my mind that George Washington would have dined at Rice Planters if the restaurant had been here when he rode through in 1791. Washington was a renowned connoisseur of fine food, and it is said that he didn't mind traveling a little out of his way to those restaurants with special skills in the culinary department.

Part of the purpose for Washington's journey to the Low Country was to study successful rice-planting techniques. Rice made its debut as an agricultural crop in the 1680s, when a ship out of Madagascar put into port at Charleston for repairs. The ship's cargo was rice, and the story goes that a peck of the grain, complete with instructions for cultivation, was sold to a local plantation owner. That rice crop produced a longer and more flavorful grain than did the typical Chinese rice, and it introduced Low Country planters to an agricultural product that helped to build great fortunes.

Rice planters became the pacesetters of their day, building magnificent plantation homes and decorating them with the finest English furnishings. It became the style to import European craftsmen for the construction of the manor houses. In fact, so close was the tie to England that rice planters were among the last to side with the colonists.

Most of the structural material at Rice Planters Restaurant was salvaged from area rice plantations and coastal warehouses. The salt-treated walls in the downstairs of the restaurant came from a Charleston warehouse. Every time the weather changes, the walls turn a different color.

My favorite place to dine at Rice Planters is the upstairs dining room that juts out over a serene creek. A frozen daiquiri turned out to be the right accompaniment for their complimentary Pepper Cheese Spread, which is addictive.

She-crab Soup is a premium item here, but my real love is the Mariner's Shrimp Creole Casserole, served with a green salad and a loaf of fresh-baked bread. Another good selection is the sautéed Onions and Chicken Livers. All true Southerners and converts will enjoy the old-fashioned Pecan Pie for dessert.

Be sure to take a tour of the facility. The restaurant pays homage to the rice planters with historical artifacts displayed in every room.

Rice Planters Restaurant is located at 6707 Kings Highway North in Myrtle Beach. Dinner is served daily from 5:00 p.m. until 10:00 p.m. For reservations, call (803) 449-3456.

RICE PLANTERS RESTAURANT'S SHE-CRAB SOUP

½ cup margarine
2 tablespoons chicken base
¾ cup self-rising flour
2 5⅓-ounce cans evaporated milk
1 quart water

2 tablespoons grated onions
1 hard-boiled egg, diced
¾ teaspoon black pepper
½ pound claw crabmeat
¼ to ½ teaspoon mace
sherry

In the top of a double boiler, place margarine, chicken base and flour. Mix to form a smooth paste. Place paste in large pot or Dutch oven and add all remaining ingredients except sherry. Cook over medium heat about 45 minutes to 1 hour, stirring frequently. More water may be added if mixture becomes too thick. Serve hot with a teaspoon of sherry added to each bowl. Yields 2 quarts.

RICE PLANTERS RESTAURANT'S
PEPPER CHEESE SPREAD

1 pound sharp cheddar cheese
4 tablespoons plus 1 teaspoon corn oil
¾ teaspoon red pepper flakes

¾ teaspoon cayenne pepper
3 tablespoons plus 1 teaspoon finely chopped banana peppers

Set out cheese until it reaches room temperature and cut into small cubes. By hand, combine the cheese with oil, red pepper flakes, cayenne pepper and banana peppers. Do not use an electric mixer. Refrigerate. Serve with saltines or Melba toast. Yields 1½ cups.

RICE PLANTERS RESTAURANT'S
MARINER'S SHRIMP CREOLE CASSEROLE

1 pound medium shrimp,
    peeled and deveined
2 tablespoons oil or butter
¼ cup chopped bell peppers
1 cup chopped onions
3 celery ribs, thinly sliced
1 clove garlic, chopped
3 tablespoons flour
1 teaspoon salt
2 teaspoons chili powder
1 teaspoon pepper
2 tablespoons sugar

¼ teaspoon sage
¼ teaspoon thyme
¼ cup green olives
½ cup canned tomatoes,
    mashed
1 cup canned small peas
1 cup chopped fresh
    mushrooms
1 cup water
rice, cooked according to
    package directions

Cook shrimp in boiling water for about 2 minutes; remove and set aside. Place oil in a skillet and sauté bell peppers, onions, celery and garlic. Place sautéed mixture in a large pot or Dutch oven. Add all remaining ingredients except shrimp and rice; cook on low heat for 45 minutes to 1 hour. Combine shrimp with sauce and serve over cooked rice. Serves 4.

SEA CAPTAIN'S HOUSE
Myrtle Beach

SEA CAPTAIN'S HOUSE

It's hard to believe that an oceanfront structure dating back to 1930 still exists in Myrtle Beach. But sure enough, snugly nestled among the multilevel buildings that seem to stretch in an endless line along the Myrtle Beach oceanfront is Sea Captain's House.

This quaint, gray-shingled cottage with the carefully tended flower beds offers welcome relief to travelers weary of neon and high-rises. Built as a vacation house for the Taylor family of High Point, North Carolina, Sea Captain's House is a nostalgic reminder of Myrtle Beach in a gentler, quieter era.

The structure began a new role as a guest house in 1954, offering nine rooms with a view and three home-cooked meals a day. By the early 1960s, travelers were beginning to develop a taste for more modern accommodations, and the guest house was sold. Although the new owners had every intention of replacing the former guest house with a high-rise hotel, a shortage of funds held off the wrecking ball. Instead, the structure was converted into a restaurant, and Sea Captain's House has continued to please the palates of locals and visitors for over twenty-five years.

It's not unusual to hear guests praise the owner's spirit of preservation when they experience the comfortable beachhouse atmosphere at Sea Captain's House. Rugged cyprus walls, original wood floors and a crackling fire in one of the entrance room's twin fireplaces offered a warm welcome on the chilly day I arrived. My table waited in the pleasant Florida Room, which served as a screened porch until Hurricane Hazel whisked away the room's supports in 1954. Today, this airy dining room with walls of knotty pine and rows of windows offers an unobstructed view of the Atlantic Ocean. It was the perfect setting for sampling the excellent midday fare at Sea Captain's House.

The South Carolina coast is known for its seafood—especially shrimp and bluefin crab—so I wasn't surprised to find the menu leaning heavily toward seafood selections. When deci-

10

sion making proved difficult, I turned my appetite over to the capable hands of the chef. There was no hesitation in his voice as he promptly recommended the Sea Island Shrimp as a starter. The tangy sweet-and-sour flavor of this delicious dish comes from a marinade, an adaptation of the pickling method used by coastal fisherman to preserve their catch before the days of refrigeration.

The Southern-style Crab Cakes were next. It was no surprise to discover that these moist, golden brown patties of sweet blue crab, served with a delicate Lemon-dill Butter, have become a signature item at Sea Captain's House. They've become so popular that they appear on the breakfast and dinner menus as well. Although I didn't think I had room for the Low Country Sea Scallops, one bite of this wonderful dish featuring tender scallops smothered in creamy Dijon Sauce convinced me that this dish was, indeed, another "must" for the recipe list.

Sea Captain's House is located at 3000 North Ocean Boulevard in Myrtle Beach. Breakfast is served from 6:00 a.m. until 10:30 a.m. daily, while lunch is served from 11:30 a.m. until 2:30 p.m. and dinner from 5:00 p.m. until 10:00 p.m. For reservations (recommended for dinner), call (803) 448-8082.

SEA CAPTAIN'S SEA ISLAND SHRIMP

3 pounds medium shrimp, cooked	**¼ cup sugar**
5 medium white onions	**2 teaspoons Tabasco sauce**
1 cup olive oil	**2 teaspoons Worcestershire sauce**
1 cup apple cider vinegar	**8 ounces small capers in liquid**
1 teaspoon salt	

Peel and devein shrimp. Peel onions and slice into paper-thin rings. Combine olive oil, vinegar, salt, sugar, Tabasco and Worcestershire in a mixing bowl. Mix with wire whisk until sugar is dissolved. Add capers and liquid. In deep, flat-bottomed, non-aluminum pan, place a layer of shrimp, then a layer of onions, alternating until all ingredients are used. Pour caper mixture over top. Cover and marinate in refrigerator overnight or at least 12 hours. Stir well before serving. Serves 6.

SEA CAPTAIN'S LOW COUNTRY
SEA SCALLOPS IN DIJON SAUCE

3½ ounces Chardonnay
2 shallots, chopped fine
1 ounce ham fat, diced fine
14 ounces half-and-half or
  cream
1 to 2 tablespoons flour
3 ounces Dijon mustard
½ teaspoon salt

½ teaspoon white pepper
4 tablespoons butter or oil
1½ pounds sea scallops
8 ounces lean country ham,
  julienned
4 ounces chopped leeks
1½ pounds cooked rice

Combine wine, shallots and ham fat in a small saucepan. Reduce over medium heat until half the volume remains. Add all except two tablespoons of the half-and-half or cream and bring to a simmer. Combine remaining half-and-half and flour and blend well into roux. Add to cream mixture, reduce heat and simmer for 15 minutes. Remove from heat and strain. Add Dijon mustard, salt and pepper. Keep sauce warm. Melt butter or heat oil in large skillet. Add scallops, ham and leeks. Cook until scallops are semi-firm and white. Add Dijon Sauce and allow to simmer over low heat for 2 minutes, heating thoroughly. Remove from heat and serve over a bed of hot rice. Serves 4 to 6.

LEE'S INLET KITCHEN
Murrells Inlet

LEE'S INLET KITCHEN

Perhaps if Lee's Inlet Kitchen had been around when legendary pirate Captain Murrell was raiding the Atlantic coast, the town of Murrells Inlet would carry a different name today. The outlaw pirate used the inlet for his base of operations and later became the town's namesake. Surely, he might have found the vittles at Lee's Inlet Kitchen so tasty that he wouldn't have left town long enough to plunder the seas.

The days of the pirates may have passed, but the marshland community of Murrells Inlet is still known for its booty of seafood treasures. The inlet's waters have been richly endowed with shrimp, crabs, oysters, clams and a variety of fish.

The structure known today as Lee's Inlet Kitchen bears little resemblance to the gas station and small store that occupied the site back in 1934. It wasn't until Eford and Pearl Lee purchased the structure in 1945 that people began arriving for fuel of a tastier sort. Although the enterprising couple opened the restaurant with only ten tables, the former gas station was destined to grow. After four decades and three generations of the Lee family's ownership and management, the restaurant has grown to four times its original size.

The lobby of the attractive gray-and-white–trimmed structure is located where old gas pumps once stood. Extensive redecorating efforts have given the entire restaurant a charming, updated look. But in the building's earliest rooms, the original interior walls still remain under the current wall treatments. A framed collection of old photographs taken during the restaurant's beginning stages hangs on the wall near the entrance.

The interior of Lee's Inlet Kitchen is comfortable in a refined manner, with blue the predominant color throughout the spacious rooms. The banks of windows, which lend a pleasant "summer porch" atmosphere to the front dining rooms, were originally provided to bring relief to customers before the days of air conditioning. Many of the wooden ladder-back chairs date to the restaurant's beginning.

Many of the seafood dishes served today at Lee's Inlet Kitchen are prepared from original family recipes that have been handed down through the generations. When it came time to order, I asked for the recommendation of the chef, who suggested that I begin my meal with an old family recipe, Green Clam Chowder. I could have made a meal of this thick brew, heavy with the distinctive flavor of fresh clams. But because I find it hard to resist shrimp, I decided to try two different dishes—Pearl Lee's Shrimp Salad and the Fried Fantail. Both preparations turned out to be excellent. I was pleasantly surprised to discover that the fantail shrimp were delightfully light and not greasy at all. Thin strips of light, batter-dipped Onion Rings were the perfect accompanying side dish.

The restaurant's impressive wine list includes an excellent selection of imported and domestic wines and beers, as well as specialty drinks and choices from the bar. When I commented on the elegantly designed menu and wine-list covers, I was told that they are the work of local artist Lee Arthur, who is also responsible for the attractive sign that hangs over the restaurant's entrance.

I truly intended to order dessert, but when the time came, I found I had not left enough room. I did, however, manage to get a peek and a whiff of some luscious slices of fresh-baked pie on their way to another table. Next time, I will definitely leave room.

Lee's Inlet Kitchen is located ½ mile south of Captain Dick's Marina on U.S. 17 Business in Murrells Inlet. Dinner is served from 5:00 p.m. until 10:00 p.m., Monday through Saturday. Reservations are not accepted except for large parties. Call (803) 651-2881 for information.

LEE'S INLET KITCHEN'S GREEN CLAM CHOWDER

2 cups potatoes, peeled and
ground
1 quart water or tomato
juice
1 stalk celery, ground
1 medium onion, ground

2 cups ground clams with
juice
salt and pepper to taste
2 to 3 slices cooked, minced
bacon with drippings

Place potatoes, water or tomato juice, celery and onion in large pot and cook over low heat for 1 hour. Add clams and clam juice and simmer for 30 minutes. Add salt and pepper and bacon with drippings. Simmer until thoroughly heated. Serve hot. Serves 4 to 6.

PEARL LEE'S SHRIMP SALAD

1 pound fresh shrimp,
boiled
4 hard-boiled eggs
¾ cup mayonnaise

2 teaspoons sweet pickle
relish
salt and pepper to taste

Peel and devein shrimp. Chop shrimp and eggs into small pieces and place in large mixing bowl. Add relish, mayonnaise and salt and pepper. Mix well. Serve on lettuce leaves with crackers. Garnish with paprika. Serves 6 to 8.

LEE'S INLET KITCHEN'S TARTAR SAUCE

1 large onion
1 large bell pepper
½ cup dill pickle relish
½ cup sweet pickle relish

1 tablespoon lemon juice
2 tablespoons
Worcestershire sauce
2 cups mayonnaise

Grind onion and pepper in food grinder, saving juices. Place mixture in medium- or large-sized bowl or pan. Add remaining ingredients and mix until thoroughly combined. Makes 3 cups.

OLIVER'S LODGE DINING ROOM
Murrells Inlet

OLIVER'S LODGE
DINING ROOM

I knew that a reference to "the real McCoy" meant that something wasn't an imitation. But I didn't realize the true significance of the phrase until I lunched at Oliver's Lodge Dining Room. The actual McCoy brothers not only lunched here but also stayed in this waterfront lodge during their rumrunning days. It was their pure, undiluted whiskey that earned the brothers a reputation for honesty. The government, however, had a different definition of honesty and sent the lawbreakers to prison.

Ironically, the McCoys' internment provided Oliver's with artistic dividends. A group of unusually fine seascapes that the brothers painted while serving time in prison now hangs in the restaurant. A perfectly rendered replica of their ship was painted on a brown paper bag, a canvas which deserves a mark for resourcefulness. As I admired the McCoys' skill, a typical Low Country meal of delicious Hush Puppies, Green Salad (with Oliver's own tangy Oil and Vinegar Dressing) and tasty Mushroom Shrimp Creole was set before me on the wooden table. The eighty-year-old table was built by Captain Mac Oliver, the lodge's first owner, who was pretty resourceful himself.

But then Oliver's has always been a testament to Low Country ingenuity. This sturdy heart-pine house was built sometime after 1860. Although current owner Maxine Oliver Hawkins says the house "looks as if it's going to fall down," it isn't. Oliver's is merely an example of authentic rusticity. As Mr. Hawkins joked, "It's the only place I know of that a coat of paint would ruin."

The interior has retained a homey atmosphere that you just don't run across in newer establishments. The collection of china and porcelain cheese keepers that belonged to Grandmother Emma Oliver is attractively arranged on antique sideboards. Little touches like these, along with the tasty, fresh fish and Corn Dodgers, are what keep customers coming back.

The day I was at Oliver's, a woman who was dining with her grandchildren stopped by and shared with me her childhood memories of visiting this old landmark. Apparently, good memories keep her coming back year after year. Another customer is the famed mystery writer Mickey Spillane, the restaurant's friend for over twenty-five years. Spillane chose this old lodge as the place where he and his bride were married.

Oliver's Lodge Dining Room is located off U.S. 17 next to Belin Methodist Church in Murrells Inlet. Dinner is served from 4:00 p.m. until 10:00 p.m., Monday through Saturday. The restaurant is open from March 15 until Thanksgiving. Reservations are not accepted, but the phone number is (803) 651-2963.

OLIVER'S LODGE DINING ROOM'S
CORN DODGERS

1 cup yellow cornmeal
¾ cup self-rising flour
½ teaspoon baking powder
½ teaspoon salt
2 tablespoons sugar

2 eggs, well beaten
1 cup milk
2 tablespoons vegetable oil
fat for deep-frying

Mix first 5 ingredients in a bowl, blending well. Add eggs, milk and oil and beat mixture well. Heat fat to 350 degrees. With your fingers, push about ½ tablespoon of dough from a spoon into deep fat, repeating until all the dough is used up. Roll the mixture over with the spoon when it pops to the surface in order to brown evenly. Remove when golden brown, usually within a minute. Place on paper towel to drain. Keep warm before serving. Serves 6 to 8.

OLIVER'S LODGE DINING ROOM'S
OIL AND VINEGAR DRESSING

½ cup cider vinegar
1 cup vegetable oil
½ tablespoon Tabasco sauce

½ tablespoon garlic powder
½ tablespoon Worcestershire
  sauce

Place all ingredients in a jar or blender and mix until thoroughly blended. Refrigerate. Shake jar before serving. Yields 1½ cups.

OLIVER'S LODGE DINING ROOM'S
MUSHROOM SHRIMP CREOLE

6 slices bacon
3 ribs thinly sliced celery
1½ large onions, chopped
1 bell pepper, chopped
1 16-ounce can tomatoes,
   mashed with juice
½ teaspoon thyme
1½ teaspoons oregano

dash of commercial hot
   sauce
salt and pepper to taste
6 large, fresh mushrooms,
   sliced
2 pounds shrimp, boiled
2 cups rice, cooked
   according to package
   directions

In a large skillet, fry bacon until crisp. Remove it from the skillet and crumble. Sauté celery, onions and pepper in bacon grease until tender. Add mashed tomatoes with juice and crumbled bacon. Stir in thyme, oregano, hot sauce and salt and pepper. Cook 1 hour on low heat, stirring often. Add mushrooms and cook for an additional 30 minutes. Add cooked shrimp to the sauce when ready to serve. Spoon creole over rice. Serves 4 to 5.

Note: Sauce and shrimp may be frozen, but they must be kept in separate containers.

PLANTERS BACK PORCH RESTAURANT
Murrells Inlet

PLANTERS BACK PORCH RESTAURANT

The house that now serves as Planters Back Porch Restaurant was built in 1887 by the Eason family. The Easons grew tobacco, cotton and corn. Their plantation was self-sustaining—they even operated a plantation store. The tobacco barn that once stood in the pecan grove survives only in an oil painting in the restaurant. The grapevines, still in arbor form, provided grapes for use in jellies, jams and wine. The pear trees provided fruit for preserves and pear relish. The garden is still tended and provides fresh vegetables in season.

Most of the planting done today occurs in the flower garden, which contains only shrubs and flowers available in the mid-1800s—most likely the same kinds that were grown in plantation days. The garden motif was chosen for the restaurant because, in days gone by, entertaining was done on the wide back porches that connected the Low Country houses with the gardens and summer kitchens in the back. Century-old pecan trees still shade the namesake porch at Planters Back Porch Restaurant. The original smokehouse remains in the garden, but it has since been attached to the main house.

The loggia-style bar overlooks the garden, and that is where I was introduced to a drink called Inlet Sunset. It's a kind of thick, orange piña colada that reminded me of the orange popsicles we used to buy from the ice cream man, although it definitely delivers more of a punch. The bar is decorated to reflect a garden setting, as are all the dining rooms. Grassy green tones underline a bevy of rich colors. These brilliant hues are set off by white latticework.

Along with a dry, light bottle of Chenin Blanc Berringer 1990, I chose the Panned Seafood Variety for dinner. This entrée is served in individual cast-iron skillets and contains lobster, lump crabmeat and shrimp in a buttery sauce. I never get enough of fresh seafood, so my dinner companions shared a delicious bite of Crabmeat au Gratin with me, and I allowed them a taste of my baked potato. Even the homemade biscuits are delightful.

Planters Back Porch offers an array of items that won't make your waistline suffer, but if you'd rather think about counting calories tomorrow, then I heartily suggest their Black Bottom Dessert Drink. This is a recipe you can whip up quickly. Then, while sitting on your porch, you can relive the entire adventure of dining at this charming old restaurant.

Planters Back Porch Restaurant is located on the corner of U.S. 17 South and Wachesaw Road in Murrells Inlet. Dinner is served from 5:00 p.m. until 10:00 p.m. daily. The restaurant is open February 15 through December 1. For reservations, call (803) 651-5263 or (803) 651-5544.

PLANTERS BACK PORCH RESTAURANT'S
BLACK BOTTOM DESSERT DRINK

1 quart chocolate ice cream
4 ounces Kahlúa
whipped cream

1 square of bittersweet
chocolate
4 maraschino cherries

Fill blender within an inch of the top with loosely packed ice cream. Add Kahlúa. Turn blender on and off quickly to remove lumps from ice cream, but do not blend until smooth. Spoon into 4 separate 16-ounce bubble glasses. Top with desired amount of whipped cream and grate chocolate over top. Add a cherry and a straw to each glass. Serves 4.

PLANTERS BACK PORCH RESTAURANT'S
INLET SUNSET

4 ounces crushed ice
2 teaspoons commercial
liquid piña colada mix
2 generous scoops orange
sherbet
1 ounce orgeat syrup

3 ounces commercial
powdered sour mix
1½ ounces vodka
whipped cream
1 maraschino cherry

23

Place crushed ice, piña colada mix, orange sherbet, orgeat syrup, sour mix and vodka in a blender container. Blend until frothy and pour into a large glass. Top with desired amount of whipped cream and a maraschino cherry. Serves 1.

PLANTERS BACK PORCH RESTAURANT'S PANNED SEAFOOD VARIETY

½ pound small shrimp, cleaned and deveined
1 pound Alaskan king crabmeat
2 pounds white backfin crabmeat

4 to 5 tablespoons cubed butter
dash of paprika
fresh parsley sprigs for garnish

In boiling water, cook shrimp for 2 minutes. Drain the shrimp and let it cool. Chop crabmeat into small lumps. Combine shrimp and crabmeat, mixing thoroughly. Grease a large cast-iron skillet or baking dish and spread mixture evenly over bottom. Dot with cubed butter. Place in a 300-degree oven for 8 to 10 minutes. Place under broiler for 1 minute. Stir to mix butter through mixture before serving. Sprinkle with paprika and garnish with parsley. Serves 8 to 10.

Note: This dish also can be prepared using chopped lobster instead of, or in addition to, shrimp.

CAPTAIN GUILDS' INN
Mount Pleasant

CAPTAIN GUILDS' INN

A hundred years ago, it was customary for people to have their businesses located in their homes for the sake of convenience. When George Lunden constructed his grocery store in Mount Pleasant in 1888, he had family living quarters built just above the store. In 1915, Captain Samuel Guilds, who operated a tugboat company in Charleston, bought the property and leased it for varied purposes for many years. The building functioned as a hardware store, a post office, a community service center and even an elementary school. A fire in the downstairs area prompted Guilds' descendants to restore the entire building in 1985.

As anyone who has done it can tell you, restoring a hundred-year-old building brings as many headaches as surprises. The old post-office boxes were found beneath the stairwell; they have been recycled for current usage. That part was fun, but having to do such things as jack up one side of the building fourteen inches or reinstall the dining-room ceiling's central medallion piece by piece were not. The dining room, painted a color called "Really Red," is decorated with floral draperies. Captain Guilds' portrait hangs above the mantel just opposite a Lexlip Hunt table. Originally, it was called a coffin table, since it opens lengthwise.

Captain Guilds' Inn offers a preset four-course meal. The evening I visited, they were serving an interesting combination of Wild Mushroom and Orange Soup, which blended a citrus flavor with a nutty mushroom taste and balanced well with crunchy Corn Fritters and chutney. A salad of Fresh Shrimp with Vinaigrette Dressing reminded me how close the coast was; it was served with healthy little Black Bean Cakes, which could have made a meal all by themselves. There were three entrées: Grouper, Duck and Atlantic Salmon. Eating healthy has never tasted so unbelievably good. My succulent salmon was ensconced in a subtle Leek Fondue, and the dish was accented with spicy Red Pepper Butter.

Before dessert, I decided to take time out and explore this attractive inn, including the added third floor. I ended up in the sunroom on the second floor, where I was served Chocolate Mousse with Essence of Cinnamon. Words can't describe its depth of richness—only tasting can! Captain Guilds' is definitely a restaurant to experience again and again.

Captain Guilds' Inn is located at 101 Pitt Street in Mount Pleasant. Lunch is served at Captain Guilds' Cafe from 11:30 a.m. until 2:30 p.m., Tuesday through Saturday. Dinner is served from 6:00 p.m. until 10:00 p.m. Sunday brunch is served from 10:00 a.m. until 2:00 p.m. For dinner reservations, call (803) 884-7009.

CAPTAIN GUILDS' INN'S ATLANTIC SALMON

Salmon:

4 tablespoons clarified butter

salt and pepper to taste

4 6-ounce salmon fillets

¼ cup white wine

Lightly salt and pepper salmon. Melt butter in large skillet and sauté fillets. Deglaze skillet with wine. When wine reduces, remove salmon and pour deglazed juices over salmon.

Red Pepper Butter:

½ pound raw butter

salt and pepper to taste

1 red pepper

1 teaspoon fresh thyme, chopped

1 teaspoon oregano, chopped

1 teaspoon fresh parsley, chopped

juice of 1 lemon

zest of 1 lemon

Soften butter to room temperature. Lightly rub red pepper with butter, sprinkle with salt and pepper. Place red pepper in a 450-degree oven and cook until skin starts to split. Remove red pepper from oven and cover with foil until cool. Peel outer skin from pepper. Dice pepper into ⅛-inch cubes. In a small bowl, mix butter, pepper and remaining ingredients until thoroughly combined. Add additional salt and pepper if desired. Lay out a sheet of 12 × 12-inch plastic wrap. Spread Red Pepper Butter onto wrap and roll into a cylinder. Refrigerate for later use.

Leek Fondue:

2 leeks	**1 cup white wine**
2 tablespoons butter	**2 cups heavy cream**
2 cups chicken stock	**salt and pepper to taste**

Trim green stems from leeks. Split white parts of leeks lengthwise and wash under cold running water to remove any soil deposits. Dice leeks into ¼-inch lengths. Melt butter in sauté pan and sauté leeks until limp. Add chicken stock and wine. Reduce slowly until ⅛ cup of liquid remains. Stir in cream; reduce until thickened. Purée mixture in food processor. Keep mixture warm in a hot-water bath. Add salt and pepper to taste.

Place Leek Fondue on each of 4 serving plates. Set salmon in center of fondue and top with Red Pepper Butter. Serves 4.

CAPTAIN GUILDS' INN'S CHOCOLATE MOUSSE WITH ESSENCE OF CINNAMON

7 ounces semisweet chocolate chips	**1 cup heavy cream**
¼ teaspoon cinnamon	**3 egg yolks**
	3 egg whites

Place chocolate chips and cinnamon in a food processor fitted with a steel blade. Blend until fine. Boil cream and pour into food processor. Blend until combined. Add egg yolks and blend thoroughly. Spoon mixture into a stainless-steel bowl and cool completely. Beat egg whites with an electric mixer until they reach a soft peak. Fold ⅓ of egg whites into chocolate mixture *gently*. Fold remaining egg whites into mixture very carefully. Cover and refrigerate for at least 4 hours. Serves 4 to 6.

82 QUEEN
Charleston

82 QUEEN

In Charleston, the best antidote for depression is a trip to 82 Queen. We had driven through a four-hour rainstorm the day we visited, and our enthusiasm was damp. But our spirits began to lift as soon as we opened the wrought-iron gate and threaded our way through the century-old courtyard into the covered patio dining area. The serenity of a private garden can lend a tranquilizing touch to most anyone's mood. And lunching opposite the arched windows secured from author Margaret Mitchell's estate added an interesting note.

After a few minutes on the plant-filled patio, Karen and I were revitalized and very hungry. The first thing we discovered was the She-crab Soup, richly spiced with sizable chunks of crabmeat. Every coastal restaurant seems to have its own special recipe for this soup, but 82 Queen's sherry-flavored She-crab is one of the best we've ever tasted.

When our salads arrived, my first impression was that they were too pretty to eat. The House Salad is a collage of romaine lettuce, mushrooms, red onion slices, alfalfa sprouts, Parmesan cheese and sourdough croutons—all topped with their delicately spiced Creamy Black Pepper Dressing. It's just as easy on the palate as their Low Country Crab Cakes, although the latter offer a heartier lunch.

The next time I'm in town, I'll dine in the upstairs dining room, which served as the main dwelling when part of the home had to be reconstructed in 1886 after the great earthquake that shook Charleston. This dining area overlooks the garden and Raw Bar adjacent to the patio. The outdoor Raw Bar, as well as the patio enclosure, can be enjoyed throughout the winter due to a clever heating system built into their overhead canopies. You never have to give up the garden atmosphere.

For dinner, there is an exciting variety of continental cuisine with Low Country overtones. An excellent choice is the Sautéed Shrimp and Scallops. The dish offers fresh shrimp and scallops in a Creamed Spinach and Tomato Sauce, served over fresh pasta. If you prefer fewer calories, the Charleston Extravaganza of lobster stuffed with crabmeat, fresh catch, shrimp and scallops will trick your weight scale. The restaurant has also started serving heart-healthy items that are approved by the medical college located in Charleston.

As its name suggests, 82 Queen is located at 82 Queen Street in Charleston. The restaurant is open every day, with full lunch served from 11:30 a.m. until 2:30 p.m. and an express lunch served from 2:30 p.m. until 3:30 p.m. Dinner is served from 6:00 p.m. until 10:00 p.m., Monday through Thursday, and from 6:00 p.m. until 10:30 p.m., Friday through Sunday. The Raw Bar opens at 5:30 p.m. For reservations (recommended for dinner and accepted for lunch parties of five or more), call (803) 723-7591.

82 QUEEN'S LOW COUNTRY CRAB CAKES

1 pound lump crabmeat	1 cup coarse breadcrumbs
½ cup mayonnaise	½ ounce fresh lemon juice
2 green onions, chopped fine	½ teaspoon ground thyme
	2 eggs
2 dashes Tabasco sauce	¼ cup half-and-half
1 dash Worcestershire sauce	butter or olive oil

Combine crabmeat, mayonnaise, onions, Tabasco, Worcestershire, ½ cup of breadcrumbs, lemon juice and thyme. Mix thoroughly. Shape mixture into patties. Beat together eggs and half-and-half. Dip patties in egg mixture and roll in remaining breadcrumbs. Sauté in butter or olive oil until golden brown. Serves 4 to 6.

82 QUEEN'S SAUTEED SHRIMP AND SCALLOPS IN CREAMED SPINACH AND TOMATO SAUCE

1½ cups margarine
1 cup flour
8 cups milk
4 cups heavy cream
2 ounces seafood base
  (available at specialty-
  food stores)
1¼ cups white wine

1 onion, diced fine
2 cups chopped spinach
1 tablespoon chopped garlic
1 cup fresh tomatoes, diced
salt and white pepper to
  taste
3 dozen peeled shrimp
3 dozen scallops

Melt 1 cup of the margarine in a large skillet. Stir in flour to make roux. Add milk, cream, seafood base, 1 cup of the white wine, onion, spinach, garlic and tomatoes. Bring to a boil, stirring constantly. Season with salt and white pepper and simmer for an additional 5 minutes. Sauté shrimp and scallops in remaining margarine and white wine. Add to cream mixture, stirring until evenly coated. Serve over bed of pasta and garnish with Parmesan cheese. Serves 10 to 12.

82 QUEEN'S TOLLHOUSE PIE

2 eggs
½ cup unsifted flour
½ cup sugar
½ cup firmly packed brown
  sugar
1 cup butter, melted and cooled
  to room temperature

1 cup semisweet chocolate
  chips
1 cup chopped walnuts
1 9-inch unbaked pie shell
whipped cream or ice cream
  (optional)
whole walnuts (optional)

Preheat oven to 325 degrees. Beat eggs in large bowl until foamy. Beat in flour, sugar and brown sugar until well blended. Blend in butter. Stir in chocolate chips and chopped walnuts. Pour into pie shell. Bake for 1 hour. Serve warm with whipped cream or ice cream. Garnish with whole walnuts if desired. Yields 1 pie.

BOCCI'S ITALIAN RESTAURANT
Charleston

BOCCI'S ITALIAN RESTAURANT

If the walls at Bocci's Italian Restaurant could talk, oh, the stories they would tell! Undoubtedly, the most entertaining tales would involve South Carolina's prohibition days of the 1890s, when a "blind tiger" was reportedly housed on the first level of this historic building. The sightless feline in question was the name given to an underground tavern, or speakeasy, which frequently operated in the back room of a grocery store.

The three-story building was built in 1868 by John Molony, a native of Ireland. The exterior reflects the popular building style of post–Civil War Charleston. The structure was designed to include a grocery store and saloon on the first floor, with living quarters on the upper levels. The building's role has changed many times since the Molony family closed the grocery in 1910, but the original structure remains intact.

Today, it houses a casual, friendly Italian restaurant with the atmosphere of a delightful neighborhood cafe, or "trattoria" of Italy. Perhaps the mismatched furnishings are the secret of the comfortable Old World feeling at Bocci's. Earthy Mexican tile floors, terra-cotta walls and a framed mural of Italian vineyards provide an interesting backdrop in the restaurant's interior, but it's the mismatched tables, chairs and Italian pottery dishes that make you feel as if you're sitting in an Italian grandmother's kitchen.

I began my feast in true Italian fashion by ordering an appetizer from the antipasti section of the menu. While my guest sang the praises of the hearty Minestrone Soup, my vote went to the Artichokes Gorgonzola, a fantastic dish featuring lightly breaded, cheese-stuffed artichokes served atop Spinach Cream Sauce.

The right wine can enhance any meal, and at Bocci's, where all the wines are Italian, it seemed only appropriate to do as the Romans do. Although my entrée choice, Lemon Basil Chicken served with pasta and subtly flavored with vermouth, could have stood alone, the crisp Chardonnay Fontanelle added a deliciously festive touch to the meal.

Because the servings at Bocci's are generously appor-
tioned and the mood is pleasantly relaxed, it's easy to forget
yourself and clean each plate set before you. I planned to skip
dessert, but my resistance evaporated when the Chocolate
Almond Cassata arrived at the table. One bite of this delicious
almond-flavored confection led to another, and like magic,
another clean plate appeared.

Bocci's Italian Restaurant is located at 158 Church Street at
the corner of Cumberland Street in Charleston. Lunch is served
from 11:30 a.m. until 3:00 p.m. daily. Dinner is served from 5:00
p.m. until 10:00 p.m., Sunday through Thursday, and from 5:00
p.m. until 11:00 p.m. on Friday and Saturday. Reservations are
not required. For information, call (803) 720-2121.

BOCCI'S ARTICHOKES GORGONZOLA
IN SPINACH CREAM SAUCE

12 large canned artichokes	1 cup milk
6 ounces ricotta cheese	2 cups all-purpose flour
6 ounces Gorgonzola cheese	2 cups Italian-seasoned
1 tablespoon lemon juice	breadcrumbs
1 egg	Parmesan cheese, grated

Heat oven to 350 degrees. Drain and core artichokes. Combine cheeses and lemon juice in a bowl, mixing well. Spoon
cheese mixture into artichokes and level. Combine egg and milk
in another bowl and mix well. Roll each artichoke in flour, then
in egg mixture and finally in breadcrumbs. Place artichokes in
baking dish. Bake about 15 to 20 minutes until well browned.

Spinach Cream Sauce:

1 cup fresh spinach	½ cup milk
2 tablespoons butter	1 teaspoon lemon juice
2 tablespoons flour	

Remove stems from spinach and discard. Melt butter in small saucepan over low heat. Add flour, stirring well. Add milk, a little at a time, stirring 3 to 5 minutes until smooth and thickened. Place spinach, white sauce and lemon juice in blender and process until smooth.

Serve artichokes on a bed of Spinach Cream Sauce and dust with Parmesan cheese. Serves 4 to 6.

BOCCI'S LEMON BASIL CHICKEN

Vermouth white sauce:

4 tablespoons butter	**⅓ cup dry vermouth**
4 tablespoons flour	**1 cube chicken bouillon**
1 tablespoon brandy	**chopped parsley to taste**
2 tablespoons cheese	**dried red pepper to taste**
1 cup heavy cream	

Melt butter in saucepan over low heat. Stir in flour and cook for 6 minutes, stirring frequently. Add remaining ingredients and continue cooking and stirring until thickened.

Chicken:

8 ounces boneless, skinless chicken breast	**1 teaspoon basil**
1 tablespoon virgin olive oil	**pinch of white pepper**
1 tablespoon fresh garlic, chopped	**1 tablespoon lemon juice**
	12 ounces angel-hair pasta, cooked and drained
1 cup sliced mushrooms	**chopped fresh parsley**
2 bunches scallions, chopped	**dried red pepper**

Cut chicken into 1-inch strips. Heat oil in sauté pan over medium heat. Add chicken and cook until lightly browned on all sides. Add garlic, mushrooms and scallions and cook until soft. Add basil, white pepper and 8 ounces of Vermouth White Sauce and cook until all ingredients are incorporated and thickened. Remove chicken and set on warmed plate. Toss pasta with sauce. Lay chicken on top of pasta and garnish with parsley and red pepper. Serve immediately. Serves 4.

CAROLINA'S
Charleston

CAROLINA'S

For some time now, I have been receiving rave reports about the restaurant rebirth at 10 Exchange Street in Charleston. Except for its pink, two-story facade, the former Perdita's is totally unrecognizable. It isn't just the uptown black-and-white decor and the oversized French posters adorning the walls of the dining room that utter a different feeling. The restaurant has changed its cuisine and its entire attitude toward food.

Perdita's was named for an actress who incited an admirer to participate in a duel. The decor was romantic and dark. The food was rich and bespoke the Old South. Now, Carolina's is a positive imprint of the New South. The bustling exuberance in the sidewalk dining room would remind me of French bistros except that Carolina's has a newer, cleaner look. Visitors might almost think they've stumbled into a California restaurant until they look at the menu. The food is heart-healthy Southern.

Carolina's still has plenty of romance, especially if you are lucky enough to reserve a table in Perdita's Room. This formal, elegant dining room has marble-textured walls, white columns and attractive print banquettes. Perdita's Room is most appropriate for guests who want a full dinner; the bistro atmosphere in the adjoining room is especially suited for people wandering in for something light after an evening's entertainment.

My guest and I were very enthusiastic about Carolina's use of Southern ingredients. Black-eyed peas have never had such zing as they do in Carolina's delicious Black-eyed Pea Cakes. And though I have never been a collards fan, I had to cheer when I tasted the restaurant's Grilled Smoked Quail Stuffed with Collard Greens and served with Tasso Grits.

But Carolina's offers more than just Southern food. Their Shrimp and Crabmeat Wontons on a ginger sauce sings its own virtues. They also do a number of great pastas and omelettes and an innovative Sante Fe Burger with Fruit Chutney, Black Beans and Carolina's Pickles. Fresh seasonal berries are offered for dessert, as is the restaurant's famous Brittle Basket Chocolate Bread Pudding with White Chocolate Mousse.

Carolina's is located at 10 Exchange Street in Charleston. Dinner is served from 5:00 p.m until 11:00 p.m., Monday through Wednesday, from 5:00 p.m. until 1:30 a.m., Thursday through Saturday, and from 5:00 p.m. until 10:00 p.m. on Sunday. Reservations for Perdita's Room are recommended well in advance. The number is (803) 724-3800.

CAROLINA'S GRILLED SMOKED QUAIL STUFFED WITH COLLARD GREENS

1 tablespoon salt
⅛ teaspoon cayenne pepper
½ teaspoon paprika
4 whole European-style deboned quails
1 bunch collards, destemmed and washed in deep, salted water (mustard or turnip greens may be substituted)

6 slices bacon, cooked and diced
¼ cup chopped onion
½ teaspoon rice vinegar
½ teaspoon sugar
pinch of cayenne pepper
sea salt (without iodine) to taste
¼ cup chicken stock or water

Mix salt, cayenne pepper and paprika and rub inside and outside of quails. Refrigerate for about 1 hour. Meanwhile, select only tender, fresh collard leaves and wash thoroughly to remove dirt and grit. Cut into ½-inch strips. Sauté bacon and onion together until bacon is cooked and onion is a light golden-brown. Add vinegar, sugar, cayenne and salt. Stir well. Add greens and chicken stock or water and simmer for about 5 minutes. More liquid may be added if needed. Taste and adjust seasonings. Stuff quails with greens until birds look plump. If a smoker is available, smoke the quails for about 5 minutes. (At this stage, they will freeze well.) If a smoker is unavailable, put about 1 inch of water in a broiler pan and place quails on a rack inside pan. Cover with a tight-fitting lid and bake at 350 degrees

39

for 30 to 40 minutes or until birds' internal temperature reaches 180 degrees. Remove from smoker or broiler and place on grill. Grill for an additional 5 minutes. Serves 4. Quails may be served with grits, a spicy gravy or fruit chutney.

THE COLONY HOUSE
Charleston

THE COLONY HOUSE

It's too bad that a city—no matter how exotic or romantic—often loses its charm after you've lived in it for a while. Karen and I are glad we don't live in Charleston, because we don't ever want this city to lose its special appeal.

As we walked past the new Pineapple Fountain in Waterfront Park on a recent visit, we saluted the Charleston spirit. The beautiful city has risen from earthquake, fire and hurricane without altering her character or gracious pace.

That is not to say that Charleston is a stranger to positive change. To my thinking, one of the most clever transitions in the city's wharf area was the conversion of the 1830s warehouse on Prioleau Street. During Charleston's golden era, this warehouse held tons of rice, indigo and cotton. All were exchanged for exotic spices and silk imports. Today, The Colony House resides behind the old warehouse's magnificent wrought-iron gates.

What I like about The Colony House is that it is a restaurant you can depend on, and there is comfort in that. It has tradition, but within that tradition are several different personalities that can accommodate any mood. For instance, we dined in the comfortable but formal front dining room, with its lace curtains and Palladian windows. Through the archway, we could see the less formal whitewashed-brick Courtyard Dining Room. Diners can also enjoy a skylit atrium not unlike one of Charleston's beautiful walled gardens. And when weather permits, the rooftop garden overlooking the harbor is used for dining. The cuisine is basically Low Country, with a heavy emphasis on seafood that is broiled or sautéed in light oils.

It was a chilly January night when we visited, so the hot and spicy Black Bean Soup was the way to go. It was accented by Lemon Poppyseed Bread, which was moist and lemony. We couldn't resist their extraordinary Crab Cakes, which were just as fresh and tangy as their reputation says. We also tried a few bites of Lobster and Scallops, served on a bed of Cilantro Cream Sauce with Red Chili Crepes, a combination that gives seafood a brand-new meaning. The Colony House's dessert cart is also hard to resist. We settled on the Sweet Potato Pecan Pie, which is a luscious combination of two Southern favorites, and Chocolate Chip Walnut Pie, which is reminiscent of darby pie with a new twist.

The Colony House is located at 35 Prioleau Street in Charleston. Lunch is served from 11:30 a.m. until 3:00 p.m., Monday through Saturday. Sunday brunch is served from 11:00 a.m. until 3:00 p.m. Dinner is served from 5:30 p.m. until 10:00 p.m., seven days a week. For reservations, call (803) 723-3424.

THE COLONY HOUSE'S
CHOCOLATE CHIP WALNUT PIE

8 ounces chocolate chips
1 10-inch pie shell
5 ounces walnuts, broken
8 ounces dark Karo syrup

2 ounces light Karo syrup
2 eggs, slightly beaten
2 tablespoons melted butter

Pour chocolate chips evenly in bottom of pie shell. Sprinkle walnuts evenly over chips. Mix syrups with eggs and melted butter, stirring until well combined. Pour over chips and walnuts. Bake in a 350-degree oven for 40 to 45 minutes. Yields 1 pie.

THE COLONY HOUSE'S BLACK BEAN SOUP

1 pound black beans
chicken stock
1 ham hock
1 teaspoon cumin
¼ teaspoon cayenne pepper
1 clove garlic, chopped
1 red onion, chopped

1 sweet red pepper, chopped
salt to taste
1 teaspoon white pepper
1 bunch cilantro, chopped
sour cream (optional)
sherry (optional)

Soak black beans overnight. Drain and rinse. Place all ingredients except sour cream and sherry in a large Dutch oven. (Use enough chicken stock to just cover beans. More stock may be

43

added if needed). Bring mixture to a boil. Cover, lower heat to simmer and cook about 45 minutes until beans are tender. Purée half of the beans in a food processor and return to pot, stirring to combine. Check and adjust seasonings. Serve with a dollop of sour cream and a teaspoon of sherry to each bowl, if desired. Serves 6 to 8.

THE COLONY HOUSE'S
SWEET POTATO PECAN PIE

1 cup cooked sweet potato
¼ cup light brown sugar
1 egg, slightly beaten
1 tablespoon heavy cream
1 tablespoon butter
1 tablespoon vanilla
¼ teaspoon salt
1 teaspoon cinnamon
⅛ teaspoon nutmeg
1 8- or 9-inch prebaked pie
 shell

¾ cup sugar
¾ cup dark corn syrup
2 eggs, slightly beaten
1½ tablespoons melted
 butter
2 teaspoons vanilla
pinch of salt
½ teaspoon cinnamon
1 cup pecans, broken

Combine first 9 ingredients and mix until well incorporated. Pour into pie shell. Combine all remaining ingredients and pour over filling in pie shell. Bake in a preheated 350-degree oven for about 40 minutes until filling is set. Yields 1 pie.

THE EAST BAY TRADING COMPANY
Charleston

THE EAST BAY TRADING COMPANY

Be prepared to be swept off your feet when you visit The East Bay Trading Company, for this three-story former warehouse built in 1880 smacks of early-American charm. A collection of treasures gathered from all over the country abounds in this one-of-a-kind restaurant, located in the heart of Charleston's historic district.

As soon as you enter the reception area on the restaurant's first floor and spot the authentic peanut-popcorn pushcart and the old-timey railroad-station bench, you will feel the urge to do some serious browsing. Why not start out, like Dawn and I did, by meandering over to the genuine San Francisco cable car, climbing in and ordering a predinner drink as you start to soak in the environment? Some of the interesting items that will catch your eye are the Gay Nineties large-wheeled bicycle that hangs over the bar area, an old-fashioned gas pump and a ten-foot-high Victorian mirror, which is located on the wall next to the "Oyster, Clam and Other Delectables Bar."

If you can drag yourself away from the entertaining first floor, fine dining awaits you on the second and third levels. Just step into the custom-built hydraulic elevator complete with glass windows and up you go—as promised, The East Bay Trading Company really does sweep you off your feet.

From the upper floors, you will have a better view of the wide-open atrium highlighted by a skylight, which allows a flood of sunlight during the day and a cozier, more intimate, under-the-stars feeling at night. Our table by the gleaming wooden railing on the second floor allowed a close-up view of the lush greenery that sprouts and tumbles from antique cooking pots suspended from the lofty ceiling.

The entertaining environment is not the only attraction at East Bay. The continental cuisine is an equal rival. We honestly didn't know where to begin with all the tempting items listed on the menu. We took the easy way out and asked the chef for his recommendations, and were we ever glad we did! For our appetizer course, we were served Escargots Bordelaise. This is an inspired creation of snails seasoned with burgundy in a succulent Bordelaise sauce. If you had been at our table, you would have thought we hadn't eaten in a week. We polished off our main courses with the same relish. My Carolina Blue Crab and Scallop Cakes were rich and spicy. Dawn's Stir-fried Vegetables disappeared in a matter of minutes.

We certainly had no business ordering dessert after cleaning every plate set before us, but who could resist Praline Crème Brûlée? We couldn't, that's for sure, and we even topped the whole meal off with cups of cappuccino piled high with whipped cream. We could hardly move. Then again, we were in no hurry to leave this wonderful restaurant.

The East Bay Trading Company is located at 161 East Bay Street on the corner of Queen Street in Charleston. Dinner is served from 5:30 p.m. until 10:30 p.m., Monday through Thursday, and from 5:30 p.m. until 11:00 p.m. on Friday and Saturday. For reservations, call (803) 722-0722.

THE EAST BAY TRADING COMPANY'S
CAROLINA BLUE CRAB AND SCALLOP CAKES

1 pound backfin crabmeat, cleaned
6 ounces scallops, cooked and chopped
1 tablespoon celery, chopped
1 tablespoon bell pepper, chopped
1 tablespoon parsley, chopped
1 tablespoon basil, chopped
1 teaspoon Dijon mustard
1 tablespoon mayonnaise

1 egg, beaten
½ cup saltine crackers, ground
3 to 4 healthy dashes Tabasco sauce
1 tablespoon Worcestershire sauce
juice of 1 lemon
1 teaspoon Old Bay Seasoning
2 to 4 tablespoons butter for sautéing

Combine all ingredients except butter in a large bowl, stirring to mix thoroughly. Shape into cakes and sauté in butter until brown on both sides. Serves 4 to 6.

THE EAST BAY TRADING COMPANY'S
PRALINE CREME BRULEE

Praline:

¼ cup sugar	1¾ cups heavy cream
4 egg yolks	1 tablespoon vanilla extract
1 teaspoon cornstarch	1 tablespoon brandy

Beat sugar, egg yolks and cornstarch to ribbon stage with an electric mixer. Bring cream to a boil in a small saucepan. Remove from heat and slowly pour into the egg yolk mixture while continuing to beat. Return mixture to saucepan and set over medium heat. Continue to stir until mixture is thick enough to coat a spoon. Do not let mixture come to a boil; using a candy thermometer, check to see that mixture does not exceed 170 degrees. Remove from heat and strain through a fine sieve. Add vanilla and brandy, stirring to completely combine. Pour into individual ramekins or dessert bowls and chill.

Topping:

¼ cup granulated sugar	¼ cup toasted almonds,
2 tablespoons water	slivered

Boil the sugar and water in a small saucepan until the sugar caramelizes. Stir in the almonds. Bring to a boil again. Pour mixture onto a marble slab or a small sheet pan. Let stand for approximately 10 minutes. Break into pieces and grind in a food processor into a coarse powder.

Top each ramekin or dessert bowl with approximately ⅛ inch of topping mixture. Serves 6.

THE FRENCH QUARTER RESTAURANT
Charleston

THE FRENCH QUARTER

The thought of an alley usually conjures up the image of a dark, mysterious and unattractive passageway. Not so at Lodge Alley. The ten-foot alley, paved with Belgian block down the middle and banked with granite on both sides, is typical of early-eighteenth-century Charleston. It's not at all dark and ugly.

Karen and I would not have known about The French Quarter Restaurant if Charleston's restaurateurs had not recommended that we investigate. Our sleuthing led to the discovery that the alley is named after a 1773 Masonic lodge where Charleston's Liberty Boys openly defied the British. On November 7, 1774, effigies of the pope, the devil, Lord North and Governor Thomas Hutchinson of Massachusetts were displayed on a "rolling stage"—or parade float—to protest the harsh treatment shown Boston.

We also discovered that the restaurant is called The French Quarter because this area was settled by French Huguenots, who arrived in 1680 with little more than their business skills and their faith.

Today's très chic Lodge Alley Inn was originally a warehouse that stored barrels of indigo, rice, salt beef and hams. It is fitting that much of the food stored there was considered exceptional, as we were told to investigate precisely because of the fine cuisine to be found there today. It's true that exceptional food can be found throughout Charleston. But no other restaurant features a giant, open rotisserie imported from France to cook lamb, squab and other meats.

We were seated in an ivory-colored dining room appointed with simplified Corinthian columns. The fresh red roses in the silver bud vase gave our white linen tablecloth the perfect splash of color. We sampled a wonderful appetizer of Oysters en Brochette, prepared with bacon and served with a creamy mustard sauce. This was followed by a very rich and subtly seasoned Shrimp Bisque.

Karen chose the Veal la Louisiane, a combination of veal and seafood in a delicate madeira sauce. I wanted to try something from the rotisserie and decided on the Swordfish au Beurre Rouge. It was fresh and basted to seduce any palate.

Their wine list includes over one hundred imported and domestic vintages, with an expected French dominance. What a decision! We chose a crisp Chardonnay that was perfect.

That old axiom "Seeing is believing" does not apply here. At the French Quarter Restaurant, tasting is believing. We shared a light Hazelnut Torte reminiscent of caramel. Ah, the French really have the last word when it comes to creamy desserts!

My own last word on this renovated eighteenth-century warehouse is "Hurray!" for the Save Charleston Foundation, which refused to allow this historic structure to be turned into high-rise condominiums.

The French Quarter Restaurant at The Lodge Alley Inn is located at 195 East Bay Street in Charleston. Meals are served daily. Breakfast is served from 7:00 a.m. until 10:30 a.m. Lunch is served from 11:30 a.m. until 2:30 p.m. Dinner is served from 6:00 p.m. until 10:00 p.m. For reservations (recommended for dinner), call (803) 722-1611.

THE FRENCH QUARTER RESTAURANT'S OYSTERS EN BROCHETTE

Beurre Blanc Sauce with Ancienne mustard:

¼ cup white wine	1 cup salted butter
¼ cup white wine vinegar	salt and white pepper to
½ tablespoon chopped	taste
shallots	1½ teaspoons Ancienne
1 small bay leaf	mustard powder
1 cup heavy cream	

In a saucepan, combine the wine, wine vinegar, shallots and bay leaf. Reduce over heat to ⅛ cup. Add cream and reduce to half. Gradually whip in small pieces of butter. Season with salt and white pepper and mustard. Remove the bay leaf. Yields 2 cups.

Oysters:

20 shelled oysters

1½ cups flour

salt and pepper to taste

3 eggs

2 cups crushed breadcrumbs

5 slices bacon

1½ cups peanut oil

Beurre Blanc Sauce with
    Ancienne mustard

Strain oysters. Season the flour with salt and pepper. Beat the eggs. Put each oyster into the flour. Shake off the excess and dip oyster in beaten eggs. Let excess egg drip off. Coat oysters with breadcrumbs and set aside. Cut bacon into square pieces. Place 5 oysters and 5 bacon pieces on each of 4 small wooden or metal skewers. Heat peanut oil in a deep fryer. Fry oysters and bacon until light brown. Serve on Beurre Blanc Sauce with Ancienne mustard. Serves 4.

THE FRENCH QUARTER RESTAURANT'S SHRIMP BISQUE

2 tablespoons butter

1 pound shrimp shells

1 small onion, diced

1 carrot, diced

½ teaspoon chopped garlic

¼ cup brandy

1 quart fish stock

1 tablespoon tomato paste

¼ cup raw rice

1 bay leaf

salt to taste

cayenne pepper to taste

4 to 6 tablespoons shrimp
    pieces

1 cup heavy cream

Melt butter in a large skillet or Dutch oven. Sauté shells, onion, carrot and garlic. Add brandy, fish stock, tomato paste, rice and bay leaf. Simmer for 1 hour. Remove bay leaf. Strain off the shells with a fine strainer. Purée rice mixture in a blender until smooth. Return to the skillet and season with salt, cayenne and shrimp pieces. Add heavy cream and heat only until blended. Serves 6 to 8.

L.A. GRILL
Charleston

L.A. GRILL

Upon entering the 1915 seamen's chapel that houses L.A. Grill, guests are almost overwhelmed with its wonderful spaciousness. Many churches today would be proud to claim the building's vaulted ceiling, which is over twenty-five feet high. The chapel was built as the Episcopal Church of the Redeemer for visiting seamen. The room that now serves as a banquet area was formerly used as a men's dormitory.

When the church was desanctified in 1967, religious symbols were removed from the stained glass. I was pleased to see that the floating anchor at the apex of the stained glass was left intact. The hand-carved ship's bow that formerly served as the pulpit is now a holding station for flambéing special dishes. A rather large replica of the painting *The Women of Amphissa* flanks one wall of the dining room. If you look carefully, you can see Bacchus, the god of wine, in the upper left-hand corner surveying the merrymaking of the vestal virgins.

My companion and I sat at the back of the chapel, which gave us a good view of the room. Semiclassical music from a pianist seated in the center of the room made dining a more intimate experience.

Each guest at L.A. Grill is given a fresh menu fastened with a gold seal. We began with Snails Florentine smothered in a delicate sauce with crunchy pine nuts and a whisper of prosciutto ham. They went perfectly with the semidry white 1982 Château Lauretan. Something I really appreciate in a restaurant is a tiny sorbet served between courses. Our first was a delicious Gelato Strawberry that cleared the path for a very unusual She-crab Soup and a simple garden salad.

For my entrée, I ordered Scallops Prosciutto, a succulent serving of scallops wrapped in prosciutto and char-broiled in a garlic-lemon butter. I swapped a few bites with my friend, who was enjoying Red Snapper topped with shrimp and a creamy wine sauce. We also sampled a few fantastic morsels of L.A. Grill's Roast Duck, which is cooked in a wood-burning oven and served with a rosemary and sage sauce.

We had eaten so much that the dessert cart brought on groans. Nonetheless, we managed to find room to indulge in a delicious Napoleon.

L.A. Grill is located at 32 Market Street in Charleston. Dinner is served from 5:00 p.m. until 10:30 p.m. For reservations (recommended), call (803) 723-3614.

L.A. GRILL'S SNAILS FLORENTINE

6 tablespoons butter	2 tablespoons pine nuts
1 dozen snails	salt and pepper to taste
2 cloves garlic, minced	⅓ cup heavy cream
1 shallot, chopped	½ cup Gruyère cheese,
4 ounces spinach, cooked	shredded

Melt butter in a skillet and sauté snails with garlic, shallot, spinach and pine nuts for 4 to 5 minutes. Add salt and pepper and sauté 1 minute more. Add cream and cheese and stir until cheese begins to melt. Place under broiler for about 1 minute. Serves 2 to 4.

L.A. GRILL'S SCALLOPS PROSCIUTTO

1½ pounds sea scallops	1½ tablespoons olive oil
8 pieces of thinly sliced	dash of garlic salt
prosciutto ham	dash of basil
3 tablespoons lemon juice	salt and pepper to taste

Wrap each scallop with prosciutto, leaving top open. Mix lemon juice with olive oil, garlic salt, basil and salt and pepper. Place wrapped scallops on a skewer. Char-broil for 3 minutes and top each scallop with lemon juice mixture. Serves 6 to 8.

L.A. GRILL'S SHE-CRAB SOUP

½ gallon milk
3 ounces flour
6 tablespoons butter
¾ pound crab roe
¾ pound crabmeat (blue
    Atlantic, if possible)

2 tablespoons salt
½ teaspoon freshly ground
    nutmeg
1 tablespoon paprika
1 teaspoon cayenne pepper
8 to 10 teaspoons sherry

Bring milk to a boil. In a skillet, stir flour and butter into a roux. Add to milk. Add crab roe, crabmeat, salt, nutmeg, paprika and cayenne pepper and bring to a boil again. Lower heat and cook for 45 minutes to 1 hour. Serve each bowl with 1 teaspoon sherry. Serves 8 to 10.

THE LIBRARY AT VENDUE INN
Charleston

THE LIBRARY
AT VENDUE INN

In French, the word vendue means "to sell." When ships docked in Charleston Harbor in the 1700s and 1800s, the area where cargo was sold became known as the French District. The level of commerce soon demanded warehouses. The district became lined with venerable brick and stone warehouses that stored indigo, grain and cotton. Today, the French District hosts the charming Vendue Inn, which was built in 1865. This European-style inn, complete with its own honor-system library, maintains one of Charleston's most elegant restaurants. That is high praise in a city of great restaurants.

The Vendue Inn reminds me of some of the quaint, personable bed-and-breakfast inns of Europe. It offers two dining rooms. My favorite is the small one with the overhanging balcony filled with good books. It is so cozy that you are tempted to curl up in a wing chair by the Adam fireplace with that book you never get around to reading at home and ring for the butler to bring a spot of tea.

Guests in the main dining room sit in Queen Anne chairs on the inn's original heart-pine floors. Passersby looking through the Palladian windows can see two massive antique crystal chandeliers, walls lined with books and a lovely old fireplace.

My guest and I chose several appetizers because they sounded so original. A good presentation always stimulates my appetite, so I was highly impressed when a red-bordered plate artistically arranged with Ricotta Dumplings in a pesto broth latticed with sliced Peppered Pheasant was set before me. It was a graceful marriage of tastes, with the pesto sauce enhancing the dumplings and drawing out the unique flavor of the meat. My guest was equally pleased with her Spicy Mustard and Barbecue Shrimp with Pickled Cucumbers. We sampled the inn's Waterzooie, which is seared quail in rich duck broth with diced foie gras, and found it delicate but not understated. I moved on to an entrée of Seared Grouper with a lively citrus and chive sauce imaginatively topped with calamari. It quickly took its place among my favorites.

The dessert menu changes frequently at the inn. All that I could manage at that point was rich vanilla ice cream accented with Bailey's Irish Cream and served in an edible, nutty, brittle bowl—it looked appealingly like a pearl resting in its shell.

True to its name, The Library at Vendue Inn satisfies like a book so good that you hate to finish.

The Library at Vendue Inn is located at 19 Vendue Range in Charleston. Dinner is served from 6:00 p.m. until 10:00 p.m., Monday through Saturday. For reservations (suggested), call (803) 577-7970.

THE LIBRARY AT VENDUE INN'S
SPICY MUSTARD AND BARBECUE SHRIMP
WITH PICKLED CUCUMBERS

Shrimp:

25 peeled and deveined shrimp
½ cup chopped onion
1 tablespoon garlic, minced
1 small jalapeño pepper, minced
2 to 3 tablespoons butter
½ cup honey

½ cup rice wine vinegar
½ cup Dijon mustard
½ cup whole-grain mustard
1 tablespoon dry mustard
1 cup chicken stock
1 teaspoon cayenne pepper
juice of 1 lemon
salt and pepper to taste

Place 6 or 7 shrimp on each of 4 skewers and keep refrigerated. Combine onion, garlic and jalapeño pepper in a medium-sized saucepan and sauté in butter until transparent. Add honey and let caramelize. Add vinegar, stirring occasionally until volume is reduced by half. Stir in mustards and chicken stock. Continue to stir until reduced to sauce consistency. Add cayenne pepper, lemon juice and salt and pepper to taste. Stir to combine. Keep warm.

Pickled Cucumbers:

2 large cucumbers, cut in
half lengthwise
½ cup white wine
½ cup rice wine vinegar
2 jalapeño peppers, sliced
and deseeded

2 tablespoons black
peppercorns
salt to taste

Snip off ends of cucumbers and discard. Combine wine, vinegar, peppers, peppercorns and salt in a medium saucepan. Bring mixture to a boil, stir and let cool. Pour mixture over cucumbers and marinate for 1 hour.

Grill shrimp, continually brushing with barbecue sauce. Place cucumbers on plates, adding a ladle of sauce around them. Add shrimp to plates and serve. Serves 4.

MAGNOLIAS
Charleston

MAGNOLIAS

When Charleston was a walled city, its original Customs House stood on the spot where Magnolias resides today. Back in 1739, this was the place where French Huguenots worked on the docks, which is how the area came to be called the French District. The old Customs House building suffered substantial damage during the 1886 earthquake and was rebuilt in 1890 as a wholesale grocery warehouse. It was renovated in 1983 as an office building. By 1989, it had become a dress shop. The present owners purchased the building from the Resolution Trust, which may be a procedure as difficult as getting into heaven.

From the sleekly dramatic black and white decor at Magnolias, it would be reasonable to assume that the food is going to be either traditional French or nouvelle, but that is not so. Rather, it's the kind of food I've been looking for over the years—I'll call it "Mama food" with an upscale touch. Their food is the kind Mama used to make. The basic ingredients are as old-fashioned as they come—grits, collard greens, salmon. But the preparation is different from anything Mama ever tried. The secret is in Magnolias' innovative mingling of different flavors, as in their Grilled Salmon over Creamy White Grits with Dill and Shallot Butter. The taste is a wonderful surprise that is both subtly tangy and richly creamy.

You'll notice that magnolias are depicted in gigantic Impressionist paintings and in wrought-iron pieces throughout the sophisticated dining rooms. I sat in the main room right below the serpentine bar. Of the restaurant's many appetizers, I'd split the blue ribbon between their hearty Skillet-seared Yellow Grits with Tasso Gravy and their Cheese-filled Roasted Red Pepper with Yellow Corn Relish and Spicy Black Beans. For a bedtime treat, I'd recommend the paper-thin French-fried potatoes baked in bleu cheese. They go well with the Napa Valley wines Magnolias offers.

At dessert time, you'll be confronted by an array of pampering "Mama food," like Cream Cheese Brownies and Lemon Pound Cake. My resistance weakened with their Banana Buttermilk Custard, which tasted like something you wish your mama had made. It was wonderful with a cup of Royal Kona Coffee. This is truly a magnificent restaurant.

Magnolias is located at 185 East Bay Street in Charleston. Meals are served from 11:00 a.m. until 11:00 p.m., Monday through Wednesday; from 11:30 a.m. until 1:00 a.m., Thursday through Saturday; and from noon until 10:00 p.m. on Sunday. For reservations (suggested), call (803) 577-7771.

MAGNOLIAS' BANANA BUTTERMILK CUSTARD

1 large banana	**¾ cup sugar**
1½ cups heavy cream	**8 egg yolks**
½ cup buttermilk	**2 teaspoons vanilla**

Preheat oven to 325 degrees. Peel the banana. Cut lengthwise, then crosswise into half-slices. Spray cooking spray inside a 1½-quart soufflé dish and line bottom with banana slices. Heat cream and buttermilk in saucepan or in top of a double boiler until hot. Add sugar, stirring until it dissolves. Beat yolks thoroughly with vanilla. Spoon a few tablespoons of the hot cream mixture into egg yolk mixture, whisking thoroughly. Slowly pour remainder of cream mixture, stirring continually. Pour combined cream and egg yolk mixture over bananas. Place soufflé dish inside a larger pot, filling larger pot with water halfway up the side of soufflé dish. Place in oven and bake for 1 hour to 1 hour and 15 minutes. Serves 6 to 7.

MAGNOLIAS' GRILLED SALMON OVER CREAMY WHITE GRITS WITH DILL AND SHALLOT BUTTER

Grits:

2 quarts chicken stock (double-strength preferred)

2½ cups coarse-ground white grits

1 cup heavy cream

salt and white pepper to taste

Bring chicken stock to a boil in a large, heavy-bottomed pot. Rinse grits and slowly stir them into the boiling chicken stock. Bring back to a boil. Lower heat and stir frequently for 25 to 30 minutes, until grits have absorbed the chicken stock and become soft. Add the cream and cook an additional 20 minutes, stirring frequently to prevent scorching. Season with salt and white pepper and keep warm in a double boiler.

Salmon:

6 4-ounce salmon filets, skinless and deboned

olive oil

salt

flour

Brush the salmon filets with olive oil. Season with salt and sprinkle very lightly with flour. Place directly onto a hot grill that has been wiped down with olive oil. Grill until done.

Dill butter:

1 pound unsalted butter

1 bunch fresh dill

2 shallots

salt and white pepper

Soften butter to room temperature. Slice dill with a sharp knife, leaving little sprigs. Add dill to butter. Mince the shallots and add to butter. Season with salt and white pepper. Roll up mixture in plastic wrap and refrigerate for 2 hours or until firm. When firm, peel away the wrap and slice butter into ¼-inch slices. Keep cold. Place grits, salmon and a slice of butter on each plate. Serves 6.

MARIANNE RESTAURANT
Charleston

MARIANNE RESTAURANT

If this popular Charleston restaurant had been named by an American with a whim for patriotic titles, it might be known today as Uncle Sam instead of Marianne. The proprietor, Serge Claire, is French born and bred, however, and he preferred to name the building after the female symbol of the republic of France.

As you might expect, the restaurant's interior is representative of the owner's homeland. But don't expect an air of formality. Instead, you'll find the easygoing attitude of Country French in this historic structure dating back to the mid-1880s.

Claire's extensive remodeling efforts have restored much of the building's original charm. The aged, English-style brick on the restaurant's exterior and interior was removed, cleaned and replaced. It was during this mammoth renovation that a star was discovered in the ceiling. Apparently, the star is the symbol of the Daughters of the Confederacy, who once occupied the building. According to Claire, the Daughters were so perturbed when they moved in and learned that the former tenants of the building were members of the Ku Klux Klan that a priest was called. The priest agreed that since the building had been a meeting place for the Klan, a blessing was in order to rid it of this taint.

The blessing was obviously well received, as Marianne Restaurant has become the "in" dining spot, especially for Le Brake Fast, a late supper that begins at 11:00 p.m. Lines form outside all the way around the corner to partake of the classic French cuisine at the popular after-theater hour.

Karen and I slipped in the side door, which opens into a most unusual bar of Japanese-lacquered ebony wood with mother-of-pearl inlays. You can look through a wrought-iron grill beside the bar into an elaborate wine cellar. Naturally, fine French wines are featured, but there are interesting continental and domestic vintages as well.

We began our meal with a French drink called a Kir Royale. It was originally the creation of a bishop in the Dijon region of France, but Claire has substituted champagne for white wine.

We then enjoyed a unique pâté, plus oysters with three preparations: Rockefeller, Bienville and Marianne. My favorite was the Marianne.

This restaurant displays its individuality in a number of clever ways, such as the hand-carved mushroom accenting my entrée of Red Snapper Marianne. This absolutely scrumptious dish could easily be a prize dieting choice, as it is poached in white wine. Just skip the cream sauce that tops the fish if you are thinking of lighter fare.

It was impossible to think of lighter fare when we saw the desserts, so we didn't even try. Instead, we shared a Mousse de Marron Christine that delivered everything its appearance promised.

Marianne Restaurant is located at 235 Meeting Street in Charleston. Dinner is served from 6:00 p.m. until 10:30 p.m., Monday through Saturday, and from 5:00 p.m. until 11:00 p.m. on Sunday. Le Brake Fast is served from 11:00 p.m. until 1:30 a.m., Monday through Saturday. For reservations (required for dinner but not accepted for Le Brake Fast), call (803) 722-7196.

MARIANNE RESTAURANT'S RED SNAPPER

Fish Fumet:

1 pound fish bones	**1 tablespoon fresh parsley**
1 ounce white wine	**1 teaspoon white pepper**
1 gallon water	**1 to 2 teaspoons salt**
1 medium onion, sliced	**½ lemon, cut up**
1 shallot, chopped	

Place fish bones in a Dutch oven and moisten with wine. Add water, onion slices, shallot, parsley, pepper, salt and lemon. Bring to a boil. Reduce heat and simmer 3 to 4 hours until liquid is reduced to ¼ of original volume. Strain bones and reserve liquid.

Sauce à la Bonne Femme:

5 tablespoons butter	**1 cup sliced mushrooms**
½ cup diced onions	**1 tablespoon lemon juice**
⅓ cup diced shallots	**1 cup white wine**
2 tablespoons flour	**salt and white pepper to**
1 cup milk	**taste**
¼ cup Fish Fumet	**½ to 1 cup heavy cream**

In a small skillet, melt 3 tablespoons of butter. Sauté onions and shallots until translucent. In a separate saucepan, combine flour and milk, stirring to make a roux. Add remaining butter to make a sauce. Add ¼ cup Fish Fumet to the sauce and stir. Add sautéed onions and shallots, mushrooms, lemon juice, wine and salt and white pepper. Let simmer 10 to 15 minutes. Stir ½ cup heavy cream into mixture and taste. Add another ½ cup for richer sauce, if desired.

Court Bullion:

1 quart Fish Fumet	**1 tablespoon lemon juice**
1 cup white wine	**4 7-ounce red snapper fillets**
1 shallot, chopped	**parsley for garnish**
1 small onion, chopped	

Place all ingredients except snapper and parsley in a large, heavy skillet on medium-high heat. Stir until ingredients are combined. Add snapper and poach a few minutes until tender and flaky. Remove snapper to warm plates and generously cover with hot Sauce à la Bonne Femme. Garnish with parsley. Serves 4.

MARIANNE RESTAURANT'S KIR ROYALE

4 to 5 ounces dry	**1 tablespoon crème de cassis**
champagne	**¼ slice orange for garnish**

In a champagne glass, combine champagne and crème de cassis. Stir. Garnish with an orange slice. Serves 1.

MIDDLETON PLACE RESTAURANT
Charleston

MIDDLETON PLACE
RESTAURANT

When I was a teenager growing up in the Southwest, I spent hours daydreaming about what it would be like to be a Southern belle and live on some far-off grand and glorious plantation. Perhaps you can understand the feelings that engulfed me, then, as I arrived at Middleton Place, a magnificent 6,500-acre antebellum plantation bordering the Ashley River. This plantation seemed to me the embodiment of my dreams.

Very few restaurants can claim a setting as romantic as Middleton Place Restaurant, located at the end of a breathtaking tour of America's oldest, and perhaps most elegant, landscaped gardens. History reports that one hundred slaves toiled for a decade to complete the terraced lawns, walks, artificial lakes and formal gardens designed in 1741 by Henry Middleton, president of the First Continental Congress. Although the historic plantation has been ravaged by war, fire and earthquake, the gardens have survived unharmed, though at times untended. No wonder the "Little Gray Lady," a disgruntled spirit sometimes seen wandering aimlessly about the neglected gardens, could find no peace until restoration efforts began in 1916.

The structure that houses the restaurant, built around 1930, is a replica of the plantation's original rice mill. A seat on the enclosed porch offers a breathtaking view of azaleas, which bloom by the thousands along the banks of Rice Mill Pond in the spring.

If you can tear your eyes away from the floral wonderland and focus on the restaurant's menu, you will find an interesting listing of plantation fare. What could be more representative of the Low Country than Hoppin' John, a typical plantation stand-by of rice, field peas and pork? Perhaps a good way to indulge your curiosity about plantation fare is to order the Low Country Sampler listed on the menu. This substantial dish features Okra Gumbo, Barbecued Pork on white rice, a Ham Biscuit, Collards, Hoppin' John and Corn Pudding. And as in any plantation kitchen, delicious homemade desserts are prepared and offered daily. I do declare—however did those Southern belles maintain such tiny waists amidst such bountiful temptations?

For those of us concerned with our own spreading waistlines, the menu offers a few light standbys. A fresh Spinach Salad, a bowl of She-crab Soup and a steaming pot of tea proved to be the perfect plantation luncheon for me.

To say I was reluctant to leave this charming restaurant—with its brick-tiled floors, cypress-paneled walls and chintz tablecloths—is an understatement. I plan to return again to Middleton Place, perhaps for one of those special antebellum dinners at which guests are made to feel as if they are dining in the aristocratic elegance of eighteenth-century plantation life.

Middleton Place Restaurant is located fourteen miles northwest of Charleston on Ashley River Road (S.C. 61). Lunch is served from 11:00 a.m. until 3:00 p.m., seven days a week. Special dinner events are also scheduled on occasion. Reservations are not accepted, but the telephone number is (803) 556-6020.

MIDDLETON PLACE RESTAURANT'S HOPPIN' JOHN

1 smoked pork jowl	1 cup raw rice
1 onion, chopped	1 teaspoon salt
6 cups water	½ teaspoon pepper
1 cup dried field peas	

Combine jowl, onion and water in a large Dutch oven. Bring to a boil, then cover and simmer over low heat for 20 minutes. Add peas. Cover and simmer for 1 hour and 45 minutes, or until peas are tender. Stir in rice, salt and pepper. Cover and simmer for 20 to 25 minutes, or until rice is tender. Yields 8 servings.

MIDDLETON PLACE RESTAURANT'S
SHRIMP SALAD

2 cups shrimp, cooked and
  cleaned
2 hard-boiled eggs, diced
2 tablespoons chopped red
  pepper
1 tablespoon chopped green
  pepper
1 cup chopped celery

1 tablespoon chopped onion
½ cup mayonnaise
1½ teaspoons salt
½ teaspoon white pepper
lettuce leaves
cucumber slices
tomato wedges

Combine shrimp, eggs, red and green peppers, celery and onion in a large bowl. Combine mayonnaise, salt and pepper. Add to shrimp mixture and toss lightly. Serve on lettuce leaves with cucumber slices and tomato wedges. Serves 4 to 6.

MIDDLETON PLACE RESTAURANT'S
CHICKEN SALAD

2 cups chicken, cooked and
  diced
½ cup diced celery
½ cup white seedless grapes
½ cup sweet pickle relish

dash of pepper
½ cup mayonnaise
lettuce leaves
chopped pecans

Combine chicken, celery, grapes, pickle relish, pepper and mayonnaise in a bowl. Stir lightly, adding seasonings if desired. Serve on lettuce leaves. Sprinkle pecans on top. Yields 6 to 8 servings.

RESTAURANT MILLION
Charleston

RESTAURANT MILLION

Since archaeologists didn't find the set of false teeth George Washington lost while dining at McCrady's Tavern in Charleston, it's doubtful that you will either. He dined in the Long Room, located just above where Restaurant Million is located today. At the opposite end of the Long Room is the oldest known theater in America, complete with a raked stage and pulleys for flying scenery. Our first president's diary entry dated May 4, 1791, recorded that "a very sumptuous dinner" was consumed here, after which artillery fire followed each of sixteen toasts.

Washington did not describe the menu, but archaeologists discovered from artifacts that this restaurant was then, as it is today, a very high-profile place to dine. During Washington's time, mutton was apparently served only in the better restaurants. So when mutton bones and wine labels from premium vintages were discovered, researchers were certain of the former tavern's character. It's especially appropriate that wine labels provided a crucial key to the archaeologists, because Phillipe Million, the creator of the new restaurant in the same location, happened to be an internationally acclaimed wine connoisseur.

The choice of a location for the new restaurant illustrates the philosophy the French have toward food—they say that the plate is to the palate what the stage is to an audience. "Fine French cooking is, in short, good theater," Million once said. What better place for a restaurant than a posh tavern that includes a stage?

In a sense, it was curtain time from the moment Karen and I entered the restaurant through the brick courtyard. We were seated opposite a dramatic 1756 Aubusson tapestry. Act One began when the crystal candelabra on our table was lighted and we were presented with a Lobster Salad flowered with beets. Color is a key element in French cuisine, and our salads were a kaleidoscope of bright hues. We wondered if the lobster could possibly taste as divine as it appeared. It did, prompting a spontaneous toast to our chefs with a Château Carbonnieux.

Action usually occurs during the second act, so we trouped back to the kitchen to watch the new, low-calorie method of preparing Breast of Duck with Bordeaux. If I'm half as skillful at home, my rendition will be the best duck my family has ever tasted. Of course, when you visit the restaurant, you don't have to do anything but sit and be pampered by the excellent food and service to thoroughly enjoy Act Two.

Act Three was a dazzling finale that is called "Symphony of Desserts." The beautifully arranged tray filled with French delicacies, exotic fruits and petite pastries was a triumph. It's the first time I've witnessed and participated in clapping for the chefs in a restaurant. Why not? It was a delicious production of nouvelle cuisine at its ultimate.

Restaurant Million is located at 2 Unity Alley in Charleston. Dinner is served from 6:30 p.m. until 10:00 p.m., Monday through Saturday. For reservations (required), call (803) 577-7472.

RESTAURANT MILLION'S
SUPREME DE CANETTE A LA LIE DU VIN
(Breast of Duck with Bordeaux)

1 4- to 5-pound duck	2 medium zucchini, sliced
1 cup red Bordeaux wine	1 10-ounce package frozen
1 teaspoon red wine vinegar	French green beans
1 cup chicken stock or	4 tablespoons butter
commercial chicken broth	2 slices bacon, minced
1 tablespoon rosemary	⅛ teaspoon basil
1 pound fresh spinach,	pinch of salt
washed, destemmed and	2 tablespoons vegetable oil
drained	4 twists white pepper
6 to 8 carrots, julienned	parsley for garnish

Puncture duck with a fork at 2- to 4-inch intervals. Roast at 350 degrees until not quite done. Meanwhile, heat wine to 80 degrees for 5 minutes. Pour the wine back into the bottle or container; the residue will separate. Skim the wine residue and place 1 cup of residue in a saucepan. Reduce over high heat until ¼ cup remains. Add red wine vinegar and reduce slightly. Add chicken stock; reduce liquids by half and set the sauce aside.

Place rosemary in boiling water. Add spinach and cook a few seconds. Remove spinach from water and set aside to drain. Add carrots, zucchini and green beans to rosemary water and steam until barely tender. Drain and set aside.

Slice roasted duck into thin strips and set aside. In a skillet, melt 1 tablespoon butter. Add bacon and sauté spinach; remove bacon and spinach from skillet. Add 1 tablespoon of butter, basil and salt to the skillet. Sauté steamed zucchini, carrots and green beans. Add the remaining 2 tablespoons of butter and the oil to the skillet, blending until mixed. Sauté the duck and remove.

Arrange duck, bacon, spinach, zucchini, carrots and green beans equally on four plates. Add a twist of white pepper to each dish. Set in a 500-degree oven for 1 minute. Remove plates from the oven and ladle Bordeaux sauce over the duck and the vegetables. Garnish with parsley. Serves 4.

NOELLE'S
Charleston

NOELLE'S

Stede Bonnet, the famous "Gentleman Pirate" who charmed the king of England into commuting his crimes, was not so lucky in 1718, when his continued piracy brought him before Chief Justice Nicholas Trott's court in Charles Town. Bonnet tried to use religion in his pleas for mercy, but Trott piously retorted that the pirate had corrupted religion instead of using it as a "lamp to your feet and light to your path." Trott then sentenced him to hang.

It was not the judgment against Stede Bonnet that irked the colonists. Rather, it was Trott's habit of codifying South Carolina laws to favor the king that led to his ouster. In 1719, the scholarly but autocratic judge retired to his home on Cumberland Street, where he applied himself to explicating the original Hebrew text of the New Testament.

Trott spent his remaining twenty-one years in the two-story brick home that now houses the Caribbean restaurant called Noelle's. Having withstood an earthquake, fires and Hurricane Hugo, the restaurant remains Charleston's oldest brick building. It is owned by Noel and Cynthia Parris, who operate it with the help of their daughters Noelle and Merle.

Nicholas Trott's portrait stared down at me from its place above the fireplace as I set about enjoying Noelle's Caribbean- and African-inspired dishes in the burgundy and white downstairs dining room. I've had so-called Caribbean food elsewhere, but it has never measured up to what I've actually eaten in the Caribbean. That all changed when I tasted Noelle's Island Pumpkin Fritters, made of puréed pumpkin and a delicious blend of herbs and spices, and their tasty Arawak Indian Fingers. Many health-conscious restaurants are serving black bean soup nowadays, but Noelle's offers an unusually gentle variation, accompanied by their own salsa and sour cream.

For my entrée, I chose the West Indian Chicken Curry with Yellow Rice. It fairly blooms with a potpourri of spices that alternates between hot and sweet but doesn't overbalance in either direction. And it's authentic, although the Barbadian chef told me that some of the dishes on the menu aren't as strong as people from her homeland usually make.

West Indians have always eaten healthy, fruit-centered desserts, so don't pass up Noelle's sorbets. My Cranberry and Pear Sorbet was a refreshing finish to an inspired meal.

Noelle's is located at 83 Cumberland Street in Charleston. Lunch is served from 11:30 a.m. until 2:00 p.m., Tuesday through Saturday. Dinner from 6:00 p.m. until 9:00 p.m., Monday through Saturday. For dinner reservations (suggested), call (803) 723-2843.

NOELLE'S WEST INDIAN CHICKEN CURRY

3 quarts water
2 chopped onions (1 small,
  1 medium)
2 celery ribs (1 halved,
  1 chopped)
1 bay leaf
2½-pound skinned and
  quartered chicken
2 medium carrots, peeled
  and diced
2 medium potatoes, peeled
  and diced

2 tablespoons olive oil
1 tablespoon curry powder
1 tablespoon ground cumin
1 tablespoon turmeric
1 tablespoon sugar
1 teaspoon dried thyme
1 teaspoon salt (optional)
1 cup chicken broth (from
  cooked chicken)
peanuts (optional)
raisins (optional)
chutney (optional)

Combine water, small onion, halved celery rib and bay leaf in heavy pot. Bring to a boil. Add chicken. Cover and simmer about 1 hour until chicken is tender. Meanwhile, pour ½ cup water into a large saucepan. Place carrots, potatoes and chopped celery in a vented basket inside large saucepan. Cover saucepan and steam for about 4 minutes. Heat olive oil in a Dutch oven. Add curry, cumin, turmeric, sugar, thyme and salt. Stir until blended. Add medium onion and sauté about 5 minutes until onion softens. Remove cooked chicken from liquid; bone and shred chicken. Skim any visible fat from broth. Strain broth, then stir 1 cup of it into curry-onion mixture. Add vegetables and chicken to sauce and stir to mix well. Cover and simmer over low heat until vegetables are tender and flavors are blended. Garnish with peanuts, raisins and chutney. Serves 6.

Note: Remaining chicken broth may be frozen for later use.

NOELLE'S YELLOW RICE

2 cups water
½ teaspoon turmeric
¼ teaspoon ginger
¼ teaspoon dry mustard
¼ teaspoon or less cayenne
   pepper

1 teaspoon salt (optional)
2 teaspoons sugar
1 cup long-grain rice

Combine all ingredients in a 3-quart saucepan with a tight-fitting lid. Bring to a boil over medium-high heat. Reduce heat until the mixture simmers, stirring with fork. Cover and simmer about 14 minutes until done. Serves 4.

NOELLE'S ISLAND PUMPKIN FRITTERS

1 cup pumpkin, cooked and
   mashed (butternut squash
   may be substituted)
½ cup milk
1 egg
1 cup all-purpose flour
1 teaspoon ground nutmeg

1 teaspoon ground
   cinnamon
½ teaspoon cayenne pepper
⅓ cup sugar
¼ teaspoon salt (optional)
1 cup vegetable oil

Combine all ingredients in large mixing bowl. Stir until well mixed and smooth. Heat vegetable oil to 375 degrees in deep fryer or heavy, deep skillet. Using greased tablespoon, drop balls of batter into hot oil, cooking 6 to 8 at a time. Cook about 4 minutes until golden brown and crisp. Drain and keep warm. Yields 15 to 20 fritters.

POOGAN'S PORCH
Charleston

POOGAN'S PORCH

Even though it was December, I sat on Poogan's front porch with a Peppermint Patty, a delicious, chocolaty cocktail. Because of the mild Charleston climate, lucky guests can enjoy the restaurant's porches throughout most of the year.

Inside, Karen joined me for lunch in a room thought to have been the parlor in this 1891 residence. The white fireplace and moldings accentuate the room's dramatic, deep-blue walls. The fresh daisies on our table and the camaraderie we noticed between waiters and guests gave this restaurant a relaxed, friendly atmosphere.

While trying to decide what to order, we decided to splurge with a bottle of Domaine Chandon champagne. I agree with the legendary creator of champagne, Dom Perignon, who said, "Champagne is like drinking stars." I've found few dishes that are not enhanced by a dry champagne.

Our sparkling wine certainly agreed with the appetizer, the succulent Crabmeat à la Poogan's. For her entrée, Karen ordered the Scallops Savannah, a wondrous creation in a mustard wine sauce. I had their Santee Catfish. If you've never tried catfish, allow Poogan's chef to introduce you to this special preparation.

Supposedly, there is a female ghost who resides in the upstairs bar, which may once have been her bedroom. We took dessert here, hoping the spirit, reportedly a small old lady dressed in a black dress with a white lace collar, would join us. Maybe we were too preoccupied with the divine Bread Pudding with Bourbon Sauce to notice her. It is said that she appears, then vanishes just as quickly without speaking a word.

We meandered out on the upstairs porch and decided that the next time we visit, we'll sit here. Perhaps we'll see Joanne Woodward and Paul Newman strolling down the lamp-lighted street. Poogan's is one of their favorite Charleston restaurants.

Poogan's Porch is located at 72 Queen Street in Charleston. Lunch is served from 11:30 a.m. until 2:30 p.m. and dinner from

5:30 p.m. until 10:30 p.m., seven days a week. For reservations (recommended), call (803) 577-2337.

POOGAN'S PORCH'S BREAD PUDDING
WITH BOURBON SAUCE

Bread Pudding:

½ loaf day-old bread	½ cup butter, melted
½ cup raisins	¾ cup sugar
1 teaspoon cinnamon	2 eggs
1 teaspoon nutmeg	2 cups milk

Break or cut bread into large chunks. Place it in a baking dish and add raisins, cinnamon, nutmeg and butter. Mix until well blended. In a small bowl, beat sugar and eggs with a whisk or electric mixer until well combined. Heat the milk, but do not boil. Add egg mixture to hot milk, mixing well. Add bread mixture and stir until will mixed. Pour everything into a greased casserole dish. Place the dish in a large roasting pan. Fill the roasting pan with water halfway up the casserole dish, taking care not to get any water in the casserole. Bake at 350 degrees for 1 hour.

Bourbon Sauce:

1 cup butter	1 egg
1 cup confectioners' sugar	2 tablespoons bourbon

Melt butter in a medium saucepan. Add sugar and cook, stirring constantly until glossy. Remove from heat. Whip in the egg with a whisk. Add the bourbon and stir until well blended. Pour about ¼ cup of sauce over each serving of Bread Pudding. Serves 4 generously.

POOGAN'S PORCH'S CRABMEAT A LA POOGAN'S

½ pound crabmeat
1 tablespoon Worcestershire sauce
1 teaspoon dry mustard
1 egg
½ of crumbled biscuit
½ teaspoon salt
½ teaspoon white pepper
1 teaspoon chopped parsley
3 tablespoons butter
8 sliced mushroom caps
4 sliced artichoke hearts
½ cup white wine
4 large biscuits or English muffins, sliced in two and toasted

Combine crabmeat, Worcestershire, mustard, egg, biscuit, salt, pepper and parsley in a bowl and mix thoroughly. Cover and refrigerate until needed. Melt butter and sauté mushrooms, artichokes and crabmeat mixture. Add white wine and mix until well blended and hot. Reduce heat until mixture thickens. Serve over toasted biscuits or muffins. Serves 4.

POOGAN'S PORCH'S PEPPERMINT PATTY

½ ounce peppermint schnapps
½ ounce Kahlúa
½ ounce crème de cacao
2 ounces heavy cream
sprig of fresh mint for garnish

Place all ingredients except the mint in a blender and mix until frothy. Serve over ice and garnish with a sprig of mint. Serves 1.

THE PRIMEROSE HOUSE
Charleston

THE PRIMEROSE HOUSE

Charleston's unique architecture has helped make her one of America's most historically important cities. A perfect example of this city's ingenuity and adaptability over the past two centuries is the "Charleston single house." The single house was designed to accommodate the deep, narrow lots of Charleston in the late 1700s. Each of the two or three stories was built one room wide and two rooms deep, with gables facing the street. Side porches, or "piazzas," extended the length of the house on the south or west side. Considered merely romantic by passersby, the piazzas were created with more than beauty in mind. Here, in the days before electric fans and air conditioning, residents found relief from the hot afternoon sun and enjoyed southeasterly sea breezes.

In 1817, Charleston auctioneer Robert Primerose added a touch of distinction to his single house on East Bay Street by constructing an elaborate semicircular portico at the front of his residence. This stately two-story brick and stucco structure was added to the National Historic Register in 1978. Today, it boasts another attractive feature—a popular restaurant on its basement level.

Although the exterior of this grand residence is anything but plain, The Primerose House is notable for its simplicity. Contemporary track lighting and terra-cotta tile floors add an interesting contrast to the original tabby walls, aged wooden doors and old fireplaces. Even the antique mahogany sculling craft suspended from a dining-room ceiling seems tailor-made for the casual, refreshing atmosphere.

Like the decor, the cuisine at The Primerose House is uncomplicated and innovative. The focus is on simple foods enhanced by fresh herbs and succulent sauces and presented with an artistic flair. Because the menu is changed every week, I can't promise that savory Herb Bread will be on the menu when you visit. But you're sure to be pleased with any of the scrumptious, warm breads that are mainstays here. Let me warn you, it took everything I had to keep myself from finishing the whole bread basket before the first course arrived.

I had heard that The Primerose House has a way with mussels, so you can imagine my delight to find Mussels with Prosciutto and Sunshine Butter on the menu. One of the secrets of this dish's success lies in the wonderful vegetable-butter sauce, which is also superb on grilled fish, chicken and vegetable dishes. The golden brown Salmon and Pea Cakes, served with an herb mayonnaise enhanced by fresh dill and a hint of garlic, also proved to be an excellent choice. I found myself applauding the chef for paying close attention to color and texture as well as taste.

Dessert was definitely not in my plan, but when the Cherry Berry Cobbler was served at a nearby table, I quickly changed my mind. How could I resist this combination of cherries, raspberries and blueberries steaming under a sinfully sweet cookie-like crust, topped with a mound of vanilla ice cream? I did the only sensible thing one can do with such a decadent dessert—I ordered a cup of freshly brewed coffee and proceeded to finish the whole thing.

The Primerose House is located at 332 East Bay Street in Charleston. Lunch is served from 11:30 a.m. until 2:00 p.m., Monday through Friday. Sunday brunch is also served from 11:30 a.m. until 2:00 p.m. Dinner is served from 6:00 p.m. until 10:00 p.m., Tuesday through Thursday, and from 6:00 p.m. until 11:00 p.m. on weekends. For reservations (recommended for dinner), call (803) 723-2954.

THE PRIMEROSE HOUSE'S MUSSELS
WITH PROSCIUTTO AND SUNSHINE BUTTER

2 dozen mussels	pinch of salt
6 ounces prosciutto, thinly sliced	chives
¼ cup sun-dried tomatoes	½ cup melted butter
½ cup cooked vegetables	splash of red wine vinegar
garlic	Parmesan cheese

Steam mussels until shells open. Remove from heat and separate shells. Remove mussels and save half of shells. Wrap slice of prosciutto around each mussel and place mussel on shell half. Process tomatoes, vegetables, garlic, salt, chives, butter and vinegar in a blender. Drizzle butter mixture over mussels and sprinkle with Parmesan cheese. Lightly brown about 2 minutes under broiler. Serves 6 to 8 as an appetizer. Leftover butter may be used for grilling fish, chicken or vegetables.

THE PRIMEROSE HOUSE'S
SALMON AND PEA CAKES

1 large onion, finely diced
1 stalk celery, finely diced
1 tablespoon butter
1 pound salmon, poached
1 tablespoon mayonnaise
8 ounces cream cheese, cut
   into cubes
3 eggs

1 teaspoon salt
juice of ½ lemon
½ teaspoon cayenne pepper
dash of Worcestershire
   sauce
1 ½ cups green peas
4 cups breadcrumbs

In large sauté pan, cook onion and celery in butter until translucent. Add salmon. Stir until salmon breaks into small pieces. Add mayonnaise and cream-cheese cubes. Stir until cheese melts. Turn off heat. Add eggs one at a time. Season with salt, lemon, cayenne and Worcestershire. Stir in peas. Add 2 cups of breadcrumbs. Form into soft patties. Press both sides of cake into remaining breadcrumbs. Deep-fry until golden brown. Serve with herb mayonnaise or mustard.

SARACEN
Charleston

SARACEN

Since the dictionary defines magnificent as "lavish, great in splendor," I'm a little skittish about using the adjective too freely. The word can be overpowering—even pretentious. Yet every time I passed Saracen's rosette windows, set in a commanding 1853–54 brownstone on East Bay Street in Charleston, it took my breath away. It wasn't until I finally stepped inside the restaurant that no other word but magnificent seemed to fit.

The former Farmers and Exchange Bank was slated for demolition back in the late 1960s when Senator Ernest F. Hollings renovated the building for his law firm. Architect Francis D. Lee built the structure in the Saracen style, a blend of Moorish and Hindu architecture that evolved from English Regency construction. The building at 141 East Bay, listed as a National Historic Landmark, is believed to be the only true example of Saracen architecture in America.

The structure was salvaged again in 1991 by Charlie Farrell. She removed the second floor, letting the main level soar past lavish windows to a skylight that accents the gold stars spattered across the night-blue ceiling and the upper walls. The effect is exotic.

You wouldn't expect barbecue in a mosque-like setting such as this, and you don't get it. What you get is Country French, elegantly prepared and presented via Farrell's culinary touch. This irrepressible young owner-chef trained in London and Paris for six years prior to transforming the building into a restaurant.

For lunch, I sampled several appetizers. The first was Venison pâté with Four-fruit Chutney. My pâté had a rich but not gamey flavor with a definite bite to it, uncommon in pâtés I've tasted. It was balanced by the vibrant chutney, which was anything but a bland accompaniment. I then tried pan-roasted Oysters with Thyme, served over toast points. Oysters have a highly distinctive taste; Farrell's sauce didn't disguise that taste but rather gave it a spirited enhancement. I tried a bit of the Roasted Pheasant with Onion and Dried Cherry Confit. It, too, was succulent, not gamey, and I found the tastes to be a proportionate blend. I also had a few nibbles of the Cheesecake with Huckleberry Sauce, which was tart and creamy and worthy of much more than a mere sampling. The same may be said of Saracen, a magnificent restaurant I plan to enjoy every time I visit Charleston.

Saracen is located at 141 East Bay Street in Charleston. Lunch is served from 11:30 a.m. until 2:30 p.m., Tuesday through Friday. Dinner is served from 6:00 p.m. until 10:30 p.m., Sunday, Tuesday, Wednesday and Thursday, with hours extended to 11:00 p.m. on Friday and Saturday. Sunday brunch is served from 11:00 a.m. until 2:30 p.m. For reservations (suggested), call (803) 723-6242.

SARACEN'S VENISON PATE

4 tablespoons butter
1 cup fresh mushrooms, sliced
½ pear, peeled, cored and sliced
½ cup celeriac (celery root), diced
⅔ cup venison, cut into chunks
¾ cup fresh pork fat, cut into chunks
½ cup pork, cut into large chunks
¾ cup red wine
1 tablespoon green peppercorns, rinsed and drained

1 bay leaf
½ tablespoon garlic, minced
¼ cup shallots, minced
¼ teaspoon celery seed
¼ cup applejack, calvados or brandy
⅓ cup venison, diced
1 egg
3 tablespoons pistachios or hazelnuts, peeled and chopped
½ to 1 tablespoon kosher salt
fresh-ground black pepper
4 to 6 slices fatty bacon

Melt butter in a skillet and sweat mushrooms, pear and celeriac until soft. Cool. Mix with chunks of venison, pork fat

91

and pork; run through fine disk of meat grinder or food processor. In a nonreactive (stainless steel or nickel) saucepan, reduce wine with peppercorns, bay leaf, garlic, shallots and celery seed to about 1 to 2 tablespoons liquid. Add brandy and flame. Cool. Discard bay leaf and most of the peppercorns. Combine ground-meat mixture with the diced venison, egg, nuts, wine reduction, salt and pepper. Fry 1 tablespoon or more to check seasoning; adjust accordingly. Line a 1½-quart terrine with bacon strips and fill with meat mixture. Cover with foil and lid. Place terrine in a larger pan and fill larger pan with water halfway up sides of terrine. Bake in a 350-degree oven for 1 hour and 15 minutes. Weight down and cool. Wrap in foil and refrigerate. Serve in thin slices. Serves 8. Freezes well.

SARACEN'S OYSTERS WITH THYME

2 to 3 tablespoons butter
2 shallots, minced
1 stalk celery, minced
pinch of cayenne pepper
½ teaspoon Tabasco sauce
1½ tablespoons fresh thyme, minced

1½ cups cream
¼ cup white wine
48 oysters
salt and pepper to taste
toast points

Melt butter and sauté shallots and celery for 1 minute. Add cayenne and sauté 1 minute longer. Add Tabasco, thyme, cream and wine; reduce sauce until slightly thickened, stirring as needed. Add oysters and simmer in sauce approximately 2 minutes, until just cooked through. Season with salt and pepper and serve over toast points. Serves 4 to 6.

TOMMY CONDON'S
Charleston

TOMMY CONDON'S If Scarlett O'Hara were around today, she could probably be found at Tommy Condon's. This engaging Irish pub and restaurant, located in a restored warehouse in Charleston's historic City Market area, would surely have taken her mind off Tara.

The interior of Tommy Condon's is a carnival of Irish delights. Walls of artifacts purchased by the owners during trips to Ireland will keep you gawking for hours. Framed Old World tapestries and a stunning tintype ceiling may add a touch of formality to the dining room, but the overall mood of this entertaining establishment is friendly, informal and definitely Irish. Is it any wonder that the South Carolina Irish Historical Society holds regular meetings here?

The most colorful part of Tommy Condon's may well be the pub, where an old, green cement trolley walk is still visible today. This historic leftover dates back to the days when hand trolley carts loaded with supplies were pushed and pulled along cement paths that wound among the warehouses in the bustling City Market area.

If the mood strikes you, take a seat at the bar and order one of Tommy Condon's famous libations. Perhaps a Leprechaun Punch or a glass of genuine Irish ale will have you singing along with the live entertainment. From your seat at the bar, you'll also have an excellent view of the richly stained beaded-board ceiling and walls. They have been restored to their original luster and provide a handsome backdrop for the antique painted mirrors and the colorful paintings of Charleston artist John Carroll Doyle.

Even though everyone is an honorary Irishman at Tommy Condon's, many homelands are represented on the menu. You'll find typical American and Low Country dishes as well as authentic Gaelic fare. The robust Shepherd's Pie, a savory beef and vegetable casserole, and the hearty Irish Potato Chowder are considered signature dishes here and should not be missed. Both of these delicious Gaelic selections are made from uncomplicated family recipes that can be reproduced in your

94

own kitchen. And as may be expected in any true Irish pub, you can bet your shillelagh that piping hot Fish and Chips will be on the menu.

Bailey's Irish Cream Cheesecake sounded wonderful for dessert, but somehow the Snickers Pie seemed the perfect finishing touch. And finish it I did, the whole sinfully sweet wedge of ice cream and candy pie. I vowed to think about dieting tomorrow, knowing that Scarlett would have understood. She would have loved Tommy Condon's, and that's no blarney!

Tommy Condon's is located at 160 Church Street in Charleston. Meals are served from 11:00 a.m. until midnight, seven days a week. As they say at Tommy Condon's, "You'll be needin' no reservations." For information, call (803) 577-3818.

TOMMY CONDON'S IRISH POTATO CHOWDER

1 tablespoon butter or margarine	¾ teaspoon seasoned salt
2 stalks celery, chopped	½ teaspoon thyme leaves
1 medium onion, chopped	½ teaspoon rosemary, crushed
3 cups hot water	¼ teaspoon garlic powder
5 chicken-flavored bouillon cubes	¼ teaspoon pepper
6 large potatoes, cubed	2 cups milk
2 carrots, peeled and sliced	1 cup shredded cheddar cheese

Melt butter in a large saucepan or soup pot over low heat. Add celery and onion and sauté about 2 to 3 minutes until onion is transparent. Add hot water and bouillon cubes, stirring to melt cubes. Add all ingredients except milk and cheese. Simmer about 20 to 30 minutes until vegetables are tender. Remove from heat. Mash vegetables with a potato masher. Add milk and cheese. Cook, stirring constantly, until cheese is melted. Serves 8 to 10.

TOMMY CONDON'S SHEPHERD'S PIE

1 pound lean top-round
  beef, cut into ½-inch
  cubes
flour for dredging
½ cup butter
1 large onion, peeled and
  diced
1 tablespoon fresh garlic,
  crushed
½ cup full-bodied red wine
2 cups water
3 carrots, peeled and cut into
  ½-inch rounds
1 cup fresh mushrooms,
  sliced

pinch of fennel
pinch of basil
pinch of oregano
pinch of thyme
pinch of salt
pinch of coarse-ground
  pepper
4 large potatoes, peeled and
  quartered
½ cup butter
pinch of nutmeg
pinch of black pepper
pinch of salt
pinch of fresh horseradish

Dredge beef in enough flour to cover all pieces completely. Shake off excess and brown beef in ½ cup of butter in a Dutch oven or a deep skillet. Add onion and cook until soft. Add garlic and wine. This mixture will thicken considerably. Add water and carrots to the beef mixture and stir to mix. Cook 15 to 20 minutes on medium heat. Add mushrooms. Continue cooking on medium heat until meat is tender. Taste and add fennel, basil, oregano, thyme, salt and coarse-ground pepper as desired. Remove from heat. Boil potatoes in enough water to cover by 2 inches. When done, immediately drain potatoes and place them in a mixing bowl with ½ cup of butter and remaining seasonings. Mash with whip or potato masher. Ladle beef mixture into casserole dishes or deep soup crocks. Spoon potatoes over beef and bake in 175-degree oven for 10 to 15 minutes until potatoes are browned and crusty. Serves 4.

THE ANCHORAGE
Beaufort

THE ANCHORAGE

When I arrived at The Anchorage, an imposing antebellum mansion overlooking the Beaufort River, I thought it a perfect setting for a historical romance. Apparently, I was not too far off the mark. In recent years, Hollywood has used Beaufort and its stately homes in the shooting of such memorable movies as *The Big Chill* and the film versions of Pat Conroy's novels *The Great Santini* and *The Prince of Tides*.

So many grand old homes abound in this lovely Low Country town that a large tract of the city has been designated a National Historic Site. One of Beaufort's most elegant mansions is The Anchorage, a three-tiered structure built in the 1770s as a summer home for a wealthy Port Royal plantation owner. This stately historic residence epitomizes the gracious lifestyle of the Old South, which changed considerably when the War Between the States fell upon the Low Country. At that time, the Union army transformed this Beaufort mansion into a hospital.

The Anchorage offers a ready-made cast of characters, including a ghost who refuses to leave the attic. Around 1891, the wealthy Admiral and Mrs. Lester Beardslee purchased the stately residence and spent some eighty thousand dollars in remodeling efforts. The result is still apparent today. The house is magnificently paneled in red oak, complete with secret wall panels that once hid the admiral's cherry-flavored liquor, which he used in making his favorite drink, called a "Cherry Bounce." His overindulgence in the spirited brew is reportedly the reason that the original circular stairway, a treacherous affair for a tipsy admiral, was replaced with the current L-shaped one. Do you suppose the ghost traipsing about the attic is none other than Mrs. Beardslee, searching for the admiral's intoxicating cache?

It is obvious that present owners Frederee and Michael Kedge cherish the lovely old home and its history and are eager to share information with their guests. They, too, have left their mark on The Anchorage with their remodeling efforts and are to be applauded for retaining the old mansion's gracious and elegant ambiance.

The Anchorage's cuisine is varied, with a menu featuring many grilled selections and seafood dishes. Each dish is carefully prepared and presented. Fresh fish and vegetables are the rule. Luncheon items always include a Seafood Platter, a wonderful Seafood Gumbo and homemade soups. Fresh salads are served with all entrées. Consider yourself fortunate if the Spinach and Grapefruit Salad with Creamy Bacon Dressing is on the menu.

Dinner selections change frequently, but maybe you'll be there when local flounder is plentiful and the Flounder Caprice is featured. This old French recipe combines delicate flounder with the sweetness of banana and crunchy toasted almonds for a memorable taste treat. Thanks to the chef, I can now create the dish in my own kitchen by following his recipe.

The Anchorage is located at 1103 Bay Street in Beaufort, across from the visitors' center. Lunch is served from 11:30 a.m. until 2:30 p.m., Monday through Friday. Dinner is served from 6:00 p.m. until 9:30 p.m., Monday through Saturday. For reservations (recommended), call (803) 524-9392.

THE ANCHORAGE'S CHERRY BOUNCE

1½ ounces vodka
1 tablespoon maraschino
  cherry juice
½ ounce cherry brandy

1 maraschino cherry
orange slice or mint for
  garnish

Fill highball glass with crushed ice and add liquid ingredients without stirring. Top with cherry and add orange slice or sprig of mint as garnish if desired. Be careful negotiating stairs after consumption! Serves 1.

THE ANCHORAGE'S FLOUNDER CAPRICE

1 banana
salt and white pepper to
taste
1 cup all-purpose flour
6- to 8-ounce flounder filet,
skinned

2 to 3 tablespoons sweet
butter
1 ounce sliced almonds
lemon for garnish

Peel and quarter banana. Add salt and white pepper to flour and mix well. Coat flounder filet and banana pieces in flour and set aside. Melt butter over gentle flame in sauté pan approximately 2 to 3 minutes until frothy. Sauté flounder until opaque, turning once. Remove flounder to ovenproof dish and place in warm oven. Increase heat under sauté pan and cook banana until lightly browned. Remove and keep warm. Add almonds and sauté until brown, stirring to avoid burning. Serve flounder garnished with banana, almonds and butter from the pan, if desired. Garnish with a lemon quarter. Serves 1 generously.

JOHN CROSS TAVERN
Beaufort

JOHN CROSS TAVERN

No, the father of our country did not sleep at John Cross Tavern, but you can be sure he was a frequent topic of conversation in this historic structure. Parson Weems, storyteller and author of *The Life of Washington*, is said to have taken his last breath here in 1825, perhaps after entertaining guests with a presidential tale.

Two restaurants can be found today in this building, which dates back to the early 1700s. Downstairs, at Harry's Restaurant, breakfast and lunch are served in an unpretentious, homey setting. This inviting room was first a mercantile store and later a schoolroom during the Revolutionary War. The lower level is named after the building's owner, Harry Chakides. He assured me that I needn't worry about the floor falling in this 250-year-old structure. When he climbed under the structure 20-plus years ago, he discovered four layers of flooring. He added two more layers, bringing the total to six. Solid footing, indeed.

John Cross Tavern occupies the upper level of the colonial building. Formerly an inn, the tavern takes its name from the man whose signature appears on the original 1717 property grant. The bar is the perfect place for predinner browsing. A glass case standing beside the original fireplace holds a collection of old bottles and clay pipes Chakides found on the grounds. I was curious about the reason for the various lengths of the pipes. He explained that it was common for the eighteenth-century smoker to simply break off a piece of pipe after each use to provide a sanitary mouthpiece for the next man.

The dining room, added to the structure during the 1970s, also contains interesting artifacts. Framed *Harper's Weekly* cartoons dating back to the 1860s line the walls and are illuminated at night by hurricane candle lamps.

My family and I noticed such unusual items on the tavern's menu as Broiled Dolphin and Fried Quail. Although we were tempted to experiment, we opted for more familiar fare. Soup was our first course, and we each felt that our own selection was the best. You will have to judge for yourself whether the She-crab Soup, the Corn Chowder or the Clam Chowder takes the prize. Next came a trip to the salad bar, where each of us put together a satisfying mound of greens and toppings. When dinner came, I noticed that my son Sean managed to polish off his Scallops and Fried Potatoes with his usual gusto. And Justin was just as thrilled with his plate of Rib-eye Steak and Fries.

We agreed to schedule our next visit to John Cross Tavern during the warm summer months, when we will be able to dine on the back terrace that overlooks the busy Beaufort River and the City Marina, a popular stopping point for Intracoastal Waterway travelers.

John Cross Tavern is located at 812 Bay Street in Beaufort. Breakfast and lunch are served at Harry's Restaurant from 6:30 a.m. until 5:00 p.m., Monday through Saturday. Dinner is served at John Cross Tavern from 5:00 p.m. until 10:00 p.m., Monday through Saturday. The lounge is open until midnight. For reservations (preferred), call (803) 524-3993.

JOHN CROSS TAVERN'S SEAFOOD ST. HELENA

6 tablespoons butter
6 tablespoons flour
3 cups milk
1 tablespoon sherry
10 ounces claw crabmeat,
    drained

10 ounces small shrimp,
    peeled and deveined
1 cup grated cheddar cheese
4 slices toasted bread

Melt butter in a saucepan over medium heat. Add flour, stirring until lump-free and blended. Add milk a little at a time and stir until mixture thickens. Add sherry and seafood. Stir until well mixed. Pour mixture into an ovenproof dish and sprinkle cheese over top. Broil until cheese starts to brown. Serve seafood with toast. Serves 4.

JOHN CROSS TAVERN'S
LOBSTER AND SHRIMP CREAM SAUCE

3 tablespoons butter
3 tablespoons flour
½ teaspoon onion salt
1½ cups milk

1 cup grated cheddar cheese
sherry to taste
½ cup lobster meat
½ cup shrimp

Melt butter in a saucepan. Stir in flour and onion salt. Add milk and cook over medium to low heat, stirring until mixture thickens. Add cheese and sherry; stir until blended. Add raw seafood and cook until thoroughly warmed. Pour over 4-ounce servings of your favorite broiled fish. (It's delicious on dolphin or swordfish.) Serves 2 generously.

JOHN CROSS TAVERN'S BLOODY MARY

1½ ounces vodka
½ ounce lemon juice
2 dashes salt
2 dashes pepper
½ ounce Worcestershire
    sauce

½ ounce hot pepper sauce
2 dashes celery salt
4 ounces tomato juice

Pour all ingredients into a shaker container and shake until well blended. Pour over ice in a 10-ounce frosted glass. Serves 1.

THE TURTLE DELI
Summerville

THE TURTLE DELI

The Turtle Deli, as its menu states, is definitely worth the search it takes to find it. It's near the center of town, in a building dating back to the late 1800s. Originally used as a general store, the structure burned to the ground a few years after construction. It was completely rebuilt in 1900 and served the community of Summerville as a variety store and meat market until 1957. It was then condemned and neglected for twenty years until Bob Porter, a local resident with an interest in preservation, began the process of renovation in 1977.

The Turtle Deli, formerly known as The Velvet Turtle, is not your common delicatessen. This cozy restaurant exudes country charm, from the blue-checked tablecloths to the intimate loft area. Wherever you sit, something of interest will catch your eye. On the walls are the Low Country scenes of renowned watercolorist Ravenel Gaillard, who makes his home in the area. A collection of miniature turtles has been donated by many regular customers who, like the restaurant's namesake, prefer the unhurried atmosphere that exists here.

If you arrive at The Turtle Deli during the warm months, you may prefer to dine alfresco in the courtyard. Giant trees provide a natural canopy in this private garden, where bamboo plants and flowering shrubs create an attractive setting.

The menu is devoted exclusively to luncheon fare and features many familiar deli selections, including hot and cold sandwiches, salads, a soup bar and a few specialty items. Quiche is a favorite, and it is delicious. Rita Corbett, the vivacious proprietor and an actress in local little-theater productions, knows the woes of the dieter. She recommends the Tuna Salad, which is served over a garden salad with special low-calorie dressing, or a cup of tasty Garden Vegetable Soup.

When it comes to dessert, however, no calories are spared. The popular Cheesecake is thick and creamy, and I doubt you'll be able to stop with one bite. The Chocolate Mocha Cake is also divine.

The Turtle Deli is located at 131 Central Avenue in Summerville. Lunch is served from 11:00 a.m. until 3:00 p.m., Monday through Saturday. Reservations are unnecessary. The telephone number is (803) 875-0380.

THE TURTLE DELI'S BROCCOLI HAM QUICHE

1 unbaked 9-inch deep-dish
  piecrust
1½ cups grated Swiss cheese
1 cup fresh or frozen
  chopped broccoli

¼ pound chopped ham
5 eggs
1 cup half-and-half

Prick the pie shell and cover the bottom with Swiss cheese. Top the cheese with broccoli and ham. In a small bowl, beat the eggs and half-and-half with a wire whisk. Pour over the ingredients in the pie shell. Bake in a 350-degree oven for 1 hour and 20 minutes. Yields 1 pie.

THE TURTLE DELI'S CHEESECAKE

¾ cup margarine
2 cups graham-cracker
  crumbs
1¾ cups sugar
2 8-ounce packages cream
  cheese, softened

⅓ cup cornstarch
16 ounces cottage cheese
4 eggs
3 tablespoons lemon juice
2 cups sour cream

Melt ¼ cup of the margarine. Mix together graham-cracker crumbs, ¼ cup of the sugar and the melted margarine. Pat into the bottom of a 10-inch springform pan and set aside. In a large bowl, combine cream cheese, remaining sugar and cornstarch, beating with an electric mixer until thoroughly blended. Put cottage cheese, eggs and lemon juice in a blender container. Blend on medium speed until well mixed. Pour into the cream cheese mixture and beat about 2 minutes with an electric mixer, until thoroughly blended. Melt the remaining ½ cup of marga-

107

rine and add to the mixture, beating well. Add sour cream and beat until blended. Pour into graham-cracker crust. Bake at 350 degrees for 1 hour. Turn off the oven and leave the cake in the oven for 2 hours. Remove the Cheesecake from the oven and allow it to remain at room temperature for an additional 2 hours before refrigerating. Yields 1 cake.

THE TURTLE DELI'S GARDEN VEGETABLE SOUP

3 quarts water
10 beef bouillon cubes
1 16-ounce can diced
   tomatoes
1 pound carrots, sliced
1 pound pole beans

2 large onions, chopped or
   sliced
2 stalks celery, chopped
1 cup corn
1 cup chopped okra
pepper to taste

Place all ingredients in a large soup pot. Bring to a boil, then turn down heat and simmer for at least 3 hours. Serves 8.

P. Faires

BONNEAU'S
Florence

BONNEAU'S

Ever wonder whether fate directs us to do even some of the simple things we do? While designing a formal English garden, Bonneau D. Lesesne found two long box planters hidden away in the 1899 Irby Mansion in Florence. It never occurred to him that it was out of the ordinary to place the planters at an unusual angle flanking the front steps—the location simply had a certain feel about it. Bonneau and his wife, Patsy, were busy transforming the former home into Florence's premier restaurant, and they never gave the planters another thought. But then a woman named Mrs. Early, who had run the home as a boardinghouse in the 1920s, brought Bonneau an exterior picture of the house made in 1929. You guessed it. The planters hadn't budged an inch!

The home was built by noted architect John L. Barringer, who included a dental sink in each bathroom. It's always amusing to see how thinking changes over the years—in those days, it wasn't considered hygienic to use the same sink for brushing your teeth and washing your face. Also, the handmade bathtubs were designed to be higher on one side, so the water wouldn't overflow. In recent years, the Lesesnes have taken great care to preserve the home's architectural integrity while embellishing it in an English style.

The Lesesnes and I dined in Chinese Chippendale chairs in the dark-stained Library Dining Room near a rose-colored marble fireplace. Anyone's appetite would perk up with the taste of Bonneau's Oysters Rockefeller, which balances the oyster-spinach duo with the restaurant's own homemade, subtly seasoned breadcrumbs. Bonneau's is also famous for their Special Salad Dressing, which is so versatile that the addition of Parmesan cheese can turn it into a dip.

Caesar salad is Caesar salad, but Bonneau's version is truly unique, owing to their homemade French-bread croutons. And why is their Veal Marsala a standout? Because they use Pro Vimi Veal and prepare it according to European techniques. The veal is sautéed in wine to impart a remarkable flavor.

110

Silky slivers of Chocolate Truffle Mousse and Bailey's Irish Cream Cake slid down with amazing speed as I sat in Bonneau's new lounge and sipped Irish coffee beneath two-hundred-year-old beams taken from slave cabins. Sitting beside the restaurant's massive, recycled fireplace is a splendid way to round out the evening.

Bonneau's is located at 231 South Irby Street in downtown Florence. Dinner is served from 6:00 p.m. until 11:00 p.m., Monday through Saturday. The restaurant is closed most major holidays. For reservations (recommended), call (803) 665-2409.

BONNEAU'S VEAL MARSALA

Garlic butter:

½ cup butter	**1 tablespoon fresh parsley,**
1 clove garlic, minced	**minced**
1 tablespoon white wine	

Soften butter and combine with remaining ingredients until well mixed.

Veal:

½ cup all-purpose flour	**8 tablespoons garlic butter**
salt and pepper to taste	**4 ounces beef bouillon**
4 4-ounce veal cutlets	**4 ounces Marsala wine**

Combine flour with salt and pepper. Pound veal with meat mallet until thin. Dust veal with seasoned flour. Heat garlic butter in skillet and sauté veal lightly. Add beef bouillon and stir until sauce begins to thicken slightly. Add wine and simmer for 5 to 7 minutes. Serves 2.

BONNEAU'S OYSTERS ROCKEFELLER

2 tablespoons garlic butter
16 oysters
½ cup spinach, thawed and
drained

½ cup provolone cheese,
grated
½ cup croutons, crushed

Soften butter and thoroughly rub into oyster cooking pan. (Muffin tins may be used instead.) Place 1 oyster in each cup. Top with equal amounts of spinach. Sprinkle equal amounts of cheese over spinach and top with croutons. Bake in a preheated 375-degree oven for 5 to 7 minutes. Serves 4.

BONNEAU'S SPECIAL SALAD DRESSING

2 cups mayonnaise
2 tablespoons lemon juice
1 large onion, chopped
1 large green pepper, seeded
and chopped

½ teaspoon salt
½ cup Parmesan cheese
(for dip only)

Place all ingredients except cheese in a blender or food processor and blend for a few minutes until well incorporated. Add cheese if making dip. Yields over 2 cups.

THE NEWTON HOUSE
Bennettsville

THE NEWTON HOUSE

When I arrived at The Newton House, I faced a difficult decision about what to have for lunch. I had heard wonderful things about their Broccoli Chowder, but the Taco Quiche was also nipping at my curiosity. Being as disciplined as always, I ordered a cup of the chowder along with the Taco Quiche. One spoonful of the thick, fresh chowder and I knew that I had made a good choice on that cool spring day. And the spicy quiche was exactly what I needed to revive my travel-weary spirits. Indeed, the restaurant has long maintained a reputation for innovative and tasty food.

The exterior of this stately Victorian home, situated on a corner near downtown Bennettsville, is painted an eye-catching Williamsburg blue. Built in 1905 for the Smith Newton family, this two-story house remained in the family until 1979, at which time it was sold and converted into a charming restaurant. Former owner Julia Ballou saw no need to change the name of the structure after the purchase. "This place had been called The Newton House for over seventy-five years, and a new name wouldn't change a thing," she reasoned.

Structurally, little changed during the transformation from residence to restaurant. Solid posts that measure four feet square run from the basement to the attic. All fireplaces are original and in working order, as is the kitchen, where current owner Jane Dupre—Julia Ballou's daughter—continues to prepare many of her mother's Yankee recipes, along with new additions of her own that delight her Confederate customers.

I originally visited The Newton House some years ago, and the biggest surprise I discovered on my return visit was the change in interior decor. The former brightly colored walls have been changed to softer tan and mauve tones, set off by white wallpaper. Though the former decor had a fun quality to it, the more muted tones feel better in this prim Victorian home. Visitors can still dine on the original closet doors, which were turned into attractive tabletops. The whimsical crates and baskets that hang from the ceiling are another longtime favorite. Even the menus themselves show a creative touch. Luncheon

114

offerings appear on a mini-newspaper, and the evening's appetizer and dinner menus are actual wine bottles.

Deft hands continue at work in the kitchen, because as daughter Jane confided, "I had the best teacher." This was proven not only with the Broccoli Chowder and the Taco Quiche, but also with the crisp green salad anointed with Vinaigrette Dressing and their irresistible presentation of bread. The Newton House does not simply serve a normal loaf or biscuit. Instead, a small crock of brown and brimming bread is placed before you. That is just one of the touches that made me want to return to this lovely restaurant again and again.

The Newton House is located at 205 McColl Street in Bennettsville. Lunch is served from 11:30 a.m. until 2:00 p.m., Monday through Friday. Dinner is served from 6:00 p.m. until 9:00 p.m., Wednesday through Friday. For reservations, call (803) 479-8173.

THE NEWTON HOUSE'S BROCCOLI CHOWDER

1 large bunch fresh broccoli	½ pound shredded Swiss
4 cups chicken broth	cheese
¾ cup half-and-half	salt and pepper to taste
2 cups milk	

Trim tough outer covering from broccoli stalks. Cut with a medium blade in a food processor until all stalks are chopped. In a soup pot, simmer broccoli stalks and florets in chicken broth until tender. Add remaining ingredients and heat slowly over low heat. Do not boil. Serves 6.

THE NEWTON HOUSE'S VINAIGRETTE DRESSING

1 cup salad oil	½ teaspoon course-ground
⅓ cup apple cider vinegar	black pepper
1 tablespoon lemon juice	salt to taste
1½ teaspoons Dijon mustard	

115

Combine all ingredients in a bowl. Whip with whisk until well blended. Shake well before serving. Yields 1½ cups.

THE NEWTON HOUSE'S TACO QUICHE

2 pounds ground beef
2 packages taco seasoning
  mix
1 10 × 15-inch sheet of
  commercial puff pastry
1½ cups onion
1½ cups chopped tomatoes

1½ cups sliced jalapeño
  peppers
1 pound or more cheddar
  cheese, shredded
10 eggs
1 cup half-and-half

Brown ground beef in a large skillet; drain thoroughly and set aside. Prepare taco seasoning mix according to package directions and stir into ground beef. Cook on medium heat for 5 to 10 minutes, stirring frequently. Line the bottom and sides of a 10 × 13-inch jelly-roll pan with puff pastry, scoring pastry with a fork. Trim sides of pastry. Pour meat mixture into crust and spread evenly over length of pan. Layer with onion, tomatoes, jalapeños and cheese. Mix eggs with half-and-half and whisk until thoroughly combined. Pour over top. Bake in a preheated 425-degree oven for 30 to 40 minutes until firm. Serves 8 to 10.

THE PADDOCK
Camden

THE PADDOCK

Some believe that the ghost of alleged Yankee carpetbagger William Daasch continues his periodic nocturnal visits to The Paddock. This restaurant is on the site where the Dutchman built his tavern, livery stable and general store in 1867. Daasch, a known tippler, is the suspected spirit whenever The Paddock's furniture is mysteriously rearranged and whenever half-empty bottles with unbroken seals are discovered in the liquor cabinet.

The original wooden building is believed to have been destroyed by fire in 1906. The Kershaw Guard Corporation, a predecessor of the National Guard, built an armory on the same spot in 1930. After the armory was sold in 1938, the building housed a packing house, an antique store and a stable. In 1977, ex-jockey Nick Butler and Skipp Achuff returned it to Daasch's original intention—a place of good food and drink. Since then, new owners Rick and Vanessa Cox have made some tasty changes in the bill of fare. But they have kept the restaurant's name and its equestrian memorabilia, since Camden plays host to two international steeplechase events. Even the "regulars" can barely wedge into The Paddock during Camden's spring Carolina Cup and the fall Colonial Cup.

The Paddock's dining room decor has a quality of refined rusticity about it, with antique burgundy velvet Louis XIV chairs, brick Roman arches and original 1866 prints. My Yankee husband, John, perked up when he saw the restaurant's import beer list. John usually chooses rib-eye or lamb chops, but I persuaded him to try the Low Country Chicken because I wanted a bite. It turned out to be a delicious, heart-healthy, spicy chicken breast served on linguini. I was also pleased to find pianist Betty Blackwell playing the old standards to accompany our lunch.

My appetizer—Crabmeat-stuffed Mushrooms—was excellent. My entrée, Halibut with Basil Sauce, was even better. The smooth, memorable sauce was the key to the halibut's succulence. And how could I possibly pass up Hot Fudge Cake on a wintry day?

The Paddock is located at 514 Rutledge Street in Camden. Lunch and dinner are served from 11:00 a.m. until 10:00 p.m., Tuesday through Friday, and from 11:00 a.m. until midnight on Saturday. For reservations, call (803) 432-3222.

THE PADDOCK'S LOW COUNTRY CHICKEN

2 chicken breasts
1 tablespoon water
½ cup butter
2 tablespoons Cajun
  seasoning
1 tablespoon fresh garlic,
  chopped
½ cup chopped green onion
  tips
¾ cup fresh mushrooms,
  sliced

¼ cup chicken stock,
  homemade or commercial
¼ cup dry white wine
linguini for 2, cooked
  according to package
  directions
¼ pound fresh asparagus,
  cooked

Pound chicken breasts with meat mallet to flatten. Cut into thin strips. Sprinkle 1 tablespoon water into heavy skillet. Heat skillet on high until beads of water dance around skillet. Add butter, stirring to melt. Stir in Cajun seasoning. Add chicken, stirring and turning until chicken is half-cooked. Add garlic, onion tips and mushrooms, stirring to incorporate. Add chicken stock and wine. Turn off heat. Place hot linguini on warmed plate and top with chicken. Garnish with asparagus. Serves 2.

THE PADDOCK'S HALIBUT WITH BASIL SAUCE

6 to 8 ounces fresh halibut
flour for dredging
salt and pepper to taste
3 to 4 tablespoons clarified
  butter
1 clove garlic, minced

4 tablespoons minced shallots
⅓ cup white wine vinegar
¾ cup fresh basil, finely
  chopped
¾ cup unsalted butter
½ cup diced tomatoes

119

Dredge halibut in flour seasoned with salt and pepper. Sauté in clarified butter and set aside in a warm place. In a saucepan, cook shallots and garlic in vinegar until the vinegar is almost completely evaporated. Add basil and a little less than ¼ cup of the unsalted butter. Whisk until the butter is almost melted, then add remaining butter. Remove from heat and add tomatoes. Season with salt and pepper. Place halibut on a warmed plate and top with sauce. Serves 2.

THE PADDOCK'S VEAL MARSALA

4 to 6 ounces escallops of veal
flour for dredging
salt and pepper
2 tablespoons olive oil
¼ cup Marsala wine
2 teaspoons tomato paste
½ cup beef stock

½ cup fresh mushrooms
¼ cup sliced green onions
2 tablespoons fresh garlic, chopped
linguini for 4, cooked according to package directions
lemon wedges

Pound veal with a meat mallet until thin. Dredge in flour seasoned with salt and pepper. Coat heavy skillet with olive oil over low to medium heat. Lightly brown veal on each side. Remove from skillet. Pour wine and tomato paste into skillet, stirring until blended. Add beef stock, mushrooms, onions and garlic. When sauce is a smooth consistency, turn heat to low and add veal to the sauce. Turn veal several times to heat through. Arrange veal on warmed plates. Warm linguini in sauce and add to plates. Garnish with lemon wedges. Serves 4.

D. Faires

CALIFORNIA DREAMING
AT UNION STATION
Columbia

CALIFORNIA DREAMING

When I learned of a historic restaurant near downtown Columbia named California Dreaming, I never expected it to be located in a former train station. The handsome, sand-colored brick structure makes quite an impression due to its sheer size. Built in 1902, the historic structure is the result of a joint effort by Southern Railway and the Atlantic Coast Line. A brick parking area with several old-timey lampposts adds the perfect nostalgic touch.

The transformation of train depot into restaurant was completed in 1983 after the building suffered almost three decades of abandonment. Today, the lively, upbeat interior of this unique building features thirteen thousand square feet of restaurant space. Various dining areas and lounges on different tiers have been cleverly designed. The expansive structure's numerous windows guarantee a bright, spacious atmosphere, capped by the lofty original ceiling, which has been sandblasted and painted white. Handsome marbleized slate floors in shades of deep green have been updated to meet today's standards.

The cuisine at California Dreaming matches the decor in casual sophistication. The dishes arrive attractively presented, well prepared, generously portioned and reasonably priced. It was no surprise to discover that this restaurant is as popular with nearby University of South Carolina students as it is with Columbia's professional uptown crowd. There's something for everyone, including a variety of salads and sandwiches, a crustless quiche, fresh seafood, barbecued and charcoal-grilled items and Mexican and Italian specialties.

The chef's choice of appetizer the afternoon I visited was the Chicken Strips Platter, a tasty, tender marvel spilling over with batter-fried strips of breast-of-chicken tenderloin. There was plenty to share with the others at my table, a habit I soon developed thanks to the generous portions.

My next selection, a heaping bowl of California Dreaming Salad served with a French honey-butter croissant, was a wonderfully fresh meal in itself. Deciding on a luncheon entrée here is a difficult task. Everything sounds wonderful, and if you're like me, just as soon as you make a decision, a waitperson glides by with some tantalizing dish that promptly leads to a change of mind.

Desserts at California Dreaming come in both solid and liquid form, so be prepared to struggle with your will power. Favorites with the sweet-tooth crowd include Snickers Pie, Apple Walnut Cinnamon Pie and the "Almost Nuts" Brownie. And regular customers have insisted that some of the liquid desserts from the bar be left on the menu no matter what. I simply couldn't resist the spirited ice-cream concoctions, either. My enjoyable afternoon ended with a sip of the restaurant's delicious Reese's Dream Cup. I was left wondering whether all of this was real or if I was merely dreaming.

California Dreaming at Union Station is located at 401 South Main Street in Columbia. Meals are served from 11:00 a.m. until 10:00 p.m., Monday through Wednesday; from 11:30 a.m. until 11:00 p.m., Thursday through Saturday; and from 11:30 a.m. to 10:00 p.m. on Sunday. Reservations are not accepted. For information, call (803) 254-6767.

CALIFORNIA DREAMING'S SPINACH SALAD

4 cups freshly chopped spinach
4 to 6 ounces commercial
   Vinaigrette, Bleu Cheese,
   Thousand Island or
   Ranch salad dressing
1 tablespoon chopped hard-
   boiled eggs
½ cup sliced mushrooms

1 tablespoon roasted
   almond slivers
1 tablespoon chopped
   bacon, hot
1 tablespoon chopped ham,
   hot
1 ripe banana, peeled and
   sliced into ½-inch sections

Place spinach into chilled salad bowl. Add dressing, followed by eggs, almonds and mushrooms. Top with bacon and ham. Place banana sections in a circular pattern to outline the contour of salad bowl. Serves 1 to 2.

CALIFORNIA DREAMING'S OMELETTE ITALIANO

2 tablespoons warm
  margarine
3 medium eggs, whipped
¼ cup chopped Italian
  sausage
½ cup sliced fresh
  mushrooms
1 cup grated mozzarella
  cheese

6 ounces tomato sauce
¼ cup sliced ripe olives
1 tablespoon chopped
  scallions
1 tablespoon grated
  Parmesan cheese
1 tablespoon sour cream

Coat bottom of Teflon pan with margarine to prevent omelette from sticking. Add eggs and cook over medium heat until outer edges of eggs become solid. Remove pan from heat. Lay sausage perpendicular to handle of pan. Add mushrooms over sausage and top with mozzarella cheese. Place pan under broiler to melt cheese. Slide omelette ⅔ of the way onto serving plate. Fold other ⅓ over, then over again. The outer omelette should have a pale-yellow appearance. Top with tomato sauce. Add olives and scallions and sprinkle Parmesan cheese over all. Place sour cream directly in center of omelette. Serves 1 generously.

CALIFORNIA DREAMING'S REESE'S DREAM CUP

1.7 ounces chilled
  Frangelico liqueur
⅔ cup chopped Reese's
  Peanut Butter Cup
8 ounces 14-percent-
  butterfat vanilla ice cream

2 heaping tablespoons
  whipped cream
1 miniature Reese's Peanut
  Butter Cup, frozen

Pour liqueur into blender. Add chopped Reese's Peanut Butter Cup and ice cream. Blend until ingredients are evenly distributed. Spoon mixture into tall glass to near top. Garnish with whipped cream and miniature Reese's Peanut Butter Cup. Serves 1 generously.

THE CAPITOL RESTAURANT
Columbia

THE CAPITOL RESTAURANT

According to Columbia lore, a certain young man seeking a circuit judgeship was informed that, if he truly wanted to be elected, he should first "score points at The Cafe." The cafe with such a powerful reputation is none other than the unpretentious black and white restaurant on Main Street.

Although The Cafe is only a half-block from the State Capitol, it doesn't seem the type of place that can make or break reputations. Perhaps that's because the restaurant's interior is humble and has remained virtually unchanged since the place opened for business in 1905. The stools still swivel under the wooden counter, while old-fashioned furnaces stand at both ends of the one-room cafe. Behind the counter are some faded photos taken after the Civil War. If you take the time to look at them, you'll be stunned at the destruction suffered by Columbia during those violent years.

No one pays attention to the fact that this place is actually The Capitol Restaurant. The name printed on the menu as well as on the National Register reads "Capitol Cafe." To the regulars, it is simply "The Cafe."

The Cafe has become known as a haven for those who are hungry for good home cooking. This restaurant caters to an interesting and unusual clientele. Legislators, government officials and mill workers can be found rubbing elbows at the counter, along with the University of South Carolina students who live in the dormitories across the street. The restaurant's twenty-four-hour schedule appeals to those who work the late shift, cram for exams or suffer from insomnia.

Current owner John Forrester continues to serve the dishes that the former proprietor, Amelia Siokis, introduced during her fifty-year reign at The Cafe. You can occasionally find Mrs. Siokis mingling with guests, some of whom are the grandchildren of her former customers.

As might be expected at a restaurant that never closes, you will find a menu listing everything from breakfast fare to midnight snacks. Other reasons for this restaurant's popularity

126

are its economical prices and hearty servings. I can imagine how much college students appreciate the oversized portions of Spaghetti with Meatballs and the bountiful Seafood Platter. A specialty of the house is the Greek Salad, a hand-me-down recipe from Mrs. Siokis. I sampled a bit of the tasty salad and a hearty Ham and Cheese Omelet that has become a favorite with night owls and students.

Watching the flow of restaurant regulars is a show in itself, but you may want to schedule your visit to The Cafe on a Tuesday night when the unnamed bluegrass band performs. On this special night, you may be able to catch the antics of some otherwise conservative legislator joining in the hootenanny with the late-night crew from the mill. It doesn't take long to understand that it's not important that the decor is not ultrachic and the cuisine less than cordon bleu. As one knowledgeable source put it, "This is simply one of the most prestigious men's clubs in town, and it costs not a penny to join."

The Capitol Restaurant is located at 1210 Main Street in Columbia. Meals are served twenty-four hours a day. Reservations are not accepted, but the phone number is (803) 765-0176.

THE CAPITOL RESTAURANT'S GREEK SALAD

1 head iceberg lettuce
2 stalks celery, diced
1 medium onion, diced
3 tomatoes, diced
2 cups crumbled feta cheese

1 2-ounce can anchovies
4 teaspoons basil
1 cup commercial oil-and-
 vinegar dressing

In a large salad bowl, break lettuce into bite-size pieces. Add celery, onion and tomatoes. Add cheese and lay anchovies over top. Sprinkle basil over all ingredients. Pour oil-and-vinegar dressing over salad before serving. Serves 6.

127

THE CAPITOL RESTAURANT'S
SPAGHETTI SAUCE

1 pound ground sirloin	1 6-ounce can tomato paste
2 tablespoons olive oil	½ teaspoon basil
½ clove minced garlic	½ teaspoon thyme
½ cup minced celery	½ teaspoon oregano
½ cup minced onion	¼ teaspoon salt
2½ cups tomato juice	2 cups beef broth

Brown the sirloin in olive oil; drain well. In a large saucepan, combine meat with all the remaining ingredients. Stir well and simmer for 2 to 3 hours until the flavors are well blended and the sauce is thick. Serve over 1 pound of spaghetti noodles cooked according to package directions. Serves 4 to 6.

THE CAPITOL RESTAURANT'S
HAM AND CHEESE OMELET

1 tablespoon oil	⅓ cup diced ham
2 eggs	salt and pepper to taste
¼ cup grated cheddar cheese	

Heat oil in a skillet. Beat the eggs and pour them into the skillet. Sprinkle cheese and ham pieces over the eggs and cook for 1 minute. Fold one side over the other; cook until eggs are lightly browned. Add salt and pepper to taste. Serves 1.

RICHARD'S
Columbia

RICHARD'S

For the past few years, the Vista community, located near the heart of downtown Columbia, has been experiencing a rebirth. Today, art galleries, sculptors' studios, antique shops and restaurants line the nooks and crannies along Gervais Street just a few blocks west of the State House.

Richard's, one of the most promising restaurants in the Vista neighborhood, is located in a prominent spot right on the corner of Gervais and Park streets. Like many buildings in the area, the two-story brick structure dates back to the turn of the century. The ten chimneys rising above the rooftop serve as reminders of the days when the building was used as a brothel, with each chimney marking the location of a former suite. Although the upper level of this handsome structure is not in use at present, there is talk of expanding the restaurant into the upstairs area. If so, visitors will once again be drawn to those old second-story suites, but this time for entertainment of the culinary variety.

The interior at Richard's is an exciting study in contrasts. The old and new have been cleverly combined to create an atmosphere that is both Victorian and contemporary. Gingerbread lace curtains and deep-green walls trimmed in creamy ivory lend an elegant, romantic touch to the various dining areas. But glowing circles of shocking-pink neon above the spacious bar prevent any semblance of stuffiness, adding instead a touch of whimsy to the otherwise refined atmosphere.

The arts flourish in the Vista neighborhood, and at Richard's they are celebrated with passion. On the evening of my visit, gorgeous serigraphs from a neighboring gallery were on display. Richard's is able to change its look often, thanks no doubt to the advantage of having several galleries located nearby. Richard's also features live music, usually a classy jazz ensemble that plays Wednesday through Sunday nights. Is it any wonder this restaurant is becoming known as the "in" place to dine in the Vista area?

Richard's specializes in fine Southern cuisine and offers one of the most exciting menus in town. Like the decor, the dishes

130

are a combination of the tried and true and the bold and new. Originality is the key here, so look for traditional dishes that come alive with the addition of something out of the ordinary. For example, tender scallops are pan-fried and served over yellow grits with Parmesan cheese sauce; fried green tomatoes and oysters are combined with a lemon-horseradish sauce; and grilled pork chops are accompanied by an apple and red pepper chutney. Whoever thinks there is nothing new under the culinary sun has never dined at Richard's.

Even the appetizers on the dinner menu are full of surprises, with such pairings as Apple Fritters with Blueberry Chutney, Scallop and Lentil Salad with Red Pepper Sauce and the excellent Peanut, Okra and Bacon Soup. Everything on the menu looked appealing. After much deliberation, I finally chose the Seafood Sausage with spicy Shrimp and Tomato Cream Sauce. This peppery and delicious dish left me begging for the recipe.

The menu at Richard's will not overwhelm you with pages of main-course selections. Instead, look for a dozen or so entrées with enticing names like Scallops, Parmesan and Yellow Corn Pasta; or Pulled Chicken on White and Yellow Grits with Dijon Cream; or Lobster and Jumbo Prawn Bouillabaisse with Onion Sausage. And each dish at Richard's is artistically presented, with as much attention paid to the eye as to the appetite. A crisp salad and fresh-baked bread are included with each entrée, and your waiter is happy to suggest the perfect wine to accompany your meal. Desserts are made fresh daily and might easily serve as a subject for another book.

Richard's is located at 936 Gervais Street at the corner of Park Street in Columbia. Lunch is served from 11:30 a.m. until 2:30 p.m., Sunday through Thursday. Dinner is served from 6:00 p.m. until 11:00 p.m., Monday through Thursday; from 6:00 p.m. until midnight on Friday and Saturday; and from 6:00 p.m. until 10:00 p.m. on Sunday. Gentlemen are requested to wear jackets. For reservations, call (803) 799-3071.

RICHARD'S SEAFOOD SAUSAGE

8 ounces fresh flounder	1 medium shallot, minced
4 ounces shrimp, peeled and deveined	1 green onion
	pinch of salt
4 ounces scallops	dash of white pepper
3 ounces clams	dash of cayenne pepper
1 egg white	½ tablespoon sesame seeds
1 tablespoon heavy cream	½ cup all-purpose flour
2 tablespoons vermouth	1 cup cooking oil

Finely chop flounder, shrimp, scallops and clams. Incorporate seafood with remaining ingredients in a medium-sized mixing bowl. Let stand in refrigerator for 30 minutes. Portion approximately 3 ounces of mix on one edge of a 12 × 12-inch sheet of plastic wrap. Roll tightly and form into sausage-sized roll, using the film at end of roll to tie off and tighten sausage. Repeat until mixture is used up. Poach in simmering water for 30 to 35 minutes. Refrigerate for 1 to 2 hours. To cook, remove wrap and dust seafood sausages lightly with flour. Heat cooking oil in medium-sized sauté pan until slightly smoking. Place sausages in oil and heat until golden brown. Turn off heat and cover for 5 minutes. Drain and serve over Shrimp and Tomato Cream Sauce.

RICHARD'S SHRIMP AND TOMATO CREAM SAUCE

1 cup picante sauce or salsa, mild or medium	1 tablespoon balsamic vinegar
12 large shrimp	2 cups heavy cream

In saucepan, reduce picante sauce, shrimp and vinegar over medium heat for 10 minutes. Remove shrimp. Add cream to picante mixture and reduce to desired consistency. May be served with pasta or Seafood Sausage.

Chef's note: Homemade salsa or picante sauce is ideal, but a quality commercial picante such as Pace also works well.

VILLA TRONCO RISTORANTE
Columbia

VILLA TRONCO
RISTORANTE

"It's called pizza. Try it, you'll like it." Nobody would order this unknown item forty years ago, so Sadie "Mama" Tronco literally had to give it away. Word spread, and before long Sadie was inundated with local customers and throngs of homesick Italian soldiers from nearby Fort Jackson. Needless to say, these soldiers were hungry for authentic Italian cooking. Such enthusiasm ensured the survival of Italian cuisine in Columbia and made a place for several generations of the Tronco family. Sadie Tronco passed away in 1987, but the restaurant continues in operation under her daughter, Carmella Tronco Martin, Carmella's husband, Henry Martin, and their children.

Every city has its own little Italian restaurant tucked away on a side street in its downtown area. Villa Tronco is Columbia's version. The restaurant's beginnings can be traced back to the early 1940s, but the building housing the restaurant dates back to the mid-1800s, when it was built for the Palmetto Fire Engine Company. Reportedly, it is the only remaining nineteenth-century firehouse in the Midland area of South Carolina. Exterior restoration took place in the summer of 1983. Layers of stucco were removed, uncovering the original brick facade. The granite plaque revealing the name of the fire-engine company and its 1858 incorporation date now hangs above the door.

The brick stable, added to the rear of the firehouse in 1903, has been converted to a two-level dining room with a skylight to give an open, airy effect. Take note of the cast-iron fire-insurance plaque that hangs near the room divider. This metal plate serves as a reminder of the days when fire protection was a conditional thing—no plaque, no protection.

The dinner menu at Villa Tronco is impressive. All items appear in Italian, with English subtitles. Whenever I think of Italian food, I think of Chianti. So I ordered a selection of the red table wine to complement my meal. My entrée was preceded by a crisp house salad topped with diced cheese, along with a small loaf of warm, fresh bread that tasted as I hoped it would—crusty on the outside and soft and chewy inside. Fortunately, my

134

entrée, Shrimp Fettuccine, arrived before I devoured the entire loaf. The plate of green and white fettuccine, tossed with cream, cheese, butter and shrimp, smelled divine and tasted as good as it looked.

I thought I wouldn't have room for dessert, but with Amaretto Cheesecake—one of "Carmella's Famous Cheesecakes"—staring me in the face, I made room. Mama mia! The cheesecake was wonderful, as was their special preparation of Caffè Cappuccino.

Another bonus at Villa Tronco is the variety of take-home items, including cheesecakes and other specialties. I later shared these purchases with my family, who proclaimed the restaurant's cuisine bravissimo!

Villa Tronco Ristorante is located at 1213 Blanding Street in Columbia. Lunch is served from 11:00 a.m. until 3:00 p.m., Monday through Saturday. Dinner is served from 5:00 p.m. until 11:00 p.m. For reservations (recommended), call (803) 256-7677.

VILLA TRONCO RISTORANTE'S
SHRIMP FETTUCCINE

½ cup butter, room temperature
½ cup grated Parmesan cheese

½ cup heavy cream
1 pound fettuccine
1 pound shrimp, boiled and deveined

In a small bowl, beat butter with a wooden spoon until creamy. Gradually add cheese and cream, beating until fluffy. Cook the fettuccine al dente. Transfer the hot, drained fettuccine onto a warm platter. Add the cream sauce and shrimp and toss until well mixed. Serves 4.

135

VILLA TRONCO RISTORANTE'S
CAFFE CAPPUCCINO

3 ounces espresso coffee
4 ounces steamed milk

dash of cinnamon
whipped cream

Brew the espresso. Pour hot espresso, steamed milk and cinnamon into a tall mug. Stir to blend. Top with whipped cream. Serves 1.

VILLA TRONCO RISTORANTE'S
PASTA WITH WHITE CLAM SAUCE

½ cup olive oil
2 cloves garlic, minced
½ cup water
1 teaspoon parsley
½ teaspoon salt

½ teaspoon oregano
½ teaspoon white pepper
2 cups whole clams with
   juice
1 pound pasta, cooked

Heat olive oil in a skillet. Add garlic and sauté until light brown in color. Slowly stir in water, parsley, salt, oregano, pepper and clams. Continue cooking over low heat until the clams are heated through. Serve over the cooked pasta. Serves 4.

THE NEWS AND HERALD TAVERN
Winnsboro

THE NEWS AND HERALD TAVERN

The News and Herald Tavern is located in a handsome building considered to be a perfect example of nineteenth-century architecture. Listed in the National Register as Thespian Hall, this impressive red brick structure gets that name from the upstairs auditorium where pre–Civil War dramas, vaudeville acts, concerts and operas were once staged. The first level of the building served as a railway station during that period.

Eventually, the building became the headquarters of Fairfield County's weekly newspaper—The News and Herald. The editorial offices occupied the premises for 139 years. Today, it's breakfast and lunch that make the headlines here.

It was gray and dismal when I arrived at the restaurant, so I was grateful for the tavern's cozy, cheerful interior. Once I set foot on the old wooden floors and took a whiff of the good, home-cooked victuals, my cloudy disposition disappeared. Old theater posters and antique props are scattered throughout the restaurant. A real show-stopper is the stained-glass panel that hangs in the front window, but my applause went to a carving of Epicurus, the Greek philosopher who was fond of good eating.

And speaking of good eating, I learned the meaning of Up Country cooking when I tasted the fruits of the culinary skills of partners Polly Parker, Betty Gutschlag and Judi Montgomery. They advised me that sandwiches are their specialty; you will find many listed on the printed menu. I chuckled at the Misprint Sandwich, their name for a sandwich that includes just about everything in the deli case. Their Chicken Salad had been highly recommended, and I found there is indeed something special about this creamy combination of chicken chunks, eggs and mayonnaise. The reason for the salad's rave reviews is said to be the addition of chicken stock. You'll be able to try it for yourself, as Polly was eager to share her secret with me.

I was surprised to find so many items listed on the menu. You will find breakfast selections as well as pastries, ice cream treats and the beer, wine and liquor that give this restaurant the right to call itself a tavern.

The tavern is located in the historic district of Winnsboro, so be sure to allow some browsing time before or after your meal. The Old Town Clock at the end of the street is said to be the oldest continuously running town clock in the United States.

The News and Herald Tavern is located at 114 East Washington Street in Winnsboro. Breakfast is served from 7:00 a.m. until 11:00 a.m. on Saturday. Breakfast and lunch are served from 7:00 a.m. until 2:00 p.m., Monday through Friday. Dinner is served from 6:00 p.m. until 9:30 p.m. on Thursday and Friday. Reservations are unnecessary, but the telephone number is (803) 635-1331.

THE NEWS AND HERALD TAVERN'S CHICKEN SALAD

1 3- to 4-pound chicken
½ cup chicken stock
2 hard-boiled eggs, chopped
2 stalks celery, chopped
½ cup chopped sweet
   pickles

½ cup mayonnaise
salt to taste
¼ teaspoon curry powder

Cover chicken with water in a soup pot and boil 1 to 1½ hours until very tender. Remove chicken from water and let cool. Reserve ½ cup of the chicken stock. Remove chicken from bones and tear into small strips. Combine chicken with stock and remaining ingredients and mix thoroughly with a wooden spoon. Serves 8 to 10.

THE NEWS AND HERALD TAVERN'S
LEMON CRUMB SQUARES

1 15-ounce can condensed milk
½ cup lemon juice
1 teaspoon grated lemon rind
1½ cups sifted all-purpose flour

1 teaspoon baking powder
½ teaspoon salt
⅔ cup butter
1 cup dark brown sugar
1 cup uncooked oatmeal

In a small bowl, combine milk, lemon juice and rind; set aside. In another bowl, sift together flour, baking powder and salt. In a large bowl, cream butter and blend in sugar. Add oatmeal and the flour mixture. Mix until crumbly. Spread ½ of the mixture in an 8 × 12 × 2-inch buttered baking pan and pat down. Spread condensed-milk mixture over top; cover with remaining crumb mixture. Bake at 350 degrees for about 25 minutes, until brown around edges. Cool in the pan at room temperature for 15 minutes. Cut into 2-inch squares and chill in the pan until firm. Yields 24 squares.

THE NEWS AND HERALD TAVERN'S
MISPRINT SANDWICH

1 8-inch hoagie roll
2 tablespoons mayonnaise
2 slices ham
2 slices cotto salami
3 slices Genoa salami
2 slices turkey
2 strips bacon, cooked
1 slice roast beef

1 slice Swiss cheese
1 slice American cheese
½ cup shredded lettuce
2 to 3 slices tomato
3 thin slices onion
1 tablespoon commercial Italian salad dressing

Split hoagie roll lengthwise. Spread mayonnaise on both sides. Alternately layer meats and cheeses. Top with lettuce, tomato and onion. Sprinkle salad dressing over all. Serves 1.

NO. 10 DOWNING STREET
Aiken

NO. 10 DOWNING STREET

No, the British prime minister doesn't live at this address, but the handsome Southern Colonial house in Aiken has all the trappings of royalty. Built around 1837, the charming structure was the residence of James Mathews Legare, poet, artist, sculptor and inventor from Charleston, who shared the historic residence with his parents. Examples of his work can be found in his former studio, the Legare Room, which was originally built on the south lawn and later attached to the house.

In 1871, the house was purchased by Thomas Morgan, a British naval officer. The distinguished residence remained in the Morgan family for over a century, until 1985, when it was sold to the present owners.

Careful attention to strict preservation standards during the restoration process is apparent in this refined restaurant today. Each of the spacious rooms contains high ceilings, original woodwork and heart-pine floors. Located within the structure are six fireplaces, each bearing a different, unique design. The fragile mantel in the Legare Room was sculpted out of preplastic cellulose, a substance invented by James Legare. Because of the mantel's historic nature, no paint is allowed to cover its original appearance.

Rose-colored walls add a touch of the romantic to your luncheon or dinner at No. 10 Downing Street. The restaurant takes its name from the little lane that is located to the side of the property. This usage of a name that is not the same as the address can be confusing for first-time visitors, but the regular patrons seem charmed by the restaurant's reference to Downing Street.

The owners, two friends and caterers, consider their restaurant's fare "fresh cuisine." But when I studied the menu, I couldn't help but feel that they were leaning toward the British Isles. The Pub Lunch, featuring Scotch Eggs and Werk Bread, seems a perfect midday meal. This popular luncheon meal can be duplicated in your own kitchen by following the recipe provided by the chef.

142

Dinner decisions at No. 10 Downing Street are anything but complicated. You'll find that the typical entrée selections include a seafood dish like Candied Salmon, prepared with wine and garlic and topped with caramelized onions, or Hawaiian Tuna, with a citrus butter sauce on angel-hair pasta.

Somehow, the menu selection of Fruit, Brie and English Biscuits served with a pot of steaming tea seems like the perfectly proper dessert in this delightful restaurant. You might want to take a leisurely stroll through the lovely English-style garden. Or if you plan a stop at the "Shoppe," you will have a chance to take home a "goodie basket" filled with delicious home-baked breads and cookies that have earned this place an impressive following.

No. 10 Downing Street is located at 241 Laurens Street in Aiken. Lunch is served Tuesday through Friday from 11:30 a.m. until 2:30 p.m., with Saturday brunch from 10:00 a.m. until 2:30 p.m. Dinner is served Tuesday through Saturday from 6:00 p.m. until 9:30 p.m. For reservations, call (803) 642-9062.

NO. 10 DOWNING STREET'S WERK BREAD

4 packages dry yeast
2 tablespoons sugar
1 cup lukewarm water
1 cup scalded milk
½ cup hot water
½ cup Guinness Stout
1 cup molasses
½ cup butter

¼ cup caraway seeds
2 tablespoons salt
4 tablespoons grated orange
    rind
2 eggs, beaten
4 cups white flour
2 cups whole-wheat flour
2 cups rye flour

Dissolve yeast and sugar in lukewarm water in small bowl. Combine milk, hot water, stout, molasses, butter, caraway seeds, salt and orange rind in large bowl. Cool to lukewarm. Add yeast mixture and eggs, mixing well. Gradually add flour and knead about 5 minutes. Place in greased bowl, cover and let rise 2 hours or until doubled in bulk. Punch down and knead 5

143

minutes. Place into 3 loaf pans, cover and let rise 2 hours or until doubled. Bake at 400 degrees for 10 minutes. Lower temperature to 350 degrees and bake for 30 minutes. Makes 3 loaves.

NO. 10 DOWNING STREET'S SCOTCH EGGS

1-pound package commercial sausage	**1 cup plain breadcrumbs**
1 cup flour	**4 large hard-boiled eggs**
2 beaten eggs	**1 to 2 cups vegetable oil**

Cut package of sausage into quarters. Place flour, beaten eggs and breadcrumbs each in a separate small bowl. With a floured hand, flatten each piece of sausage and wrap it around hard-boiled egg. Roll in flour, covering evenly. Roll in egg mixture, then in crumbs. Heat oil to 350 degrees and deep-fry eggs in hot oil for 8 minutes. Drain on paper towels and refrigerate until chilled. Serve cut in half on a bed of lettuce. Serves 4.

NO. 10 DOWNING STREET'S
LEEK AND POTATO SOUP

6 large leeks	**1 quart chicken stock**
1 jumbo yellow onion	**6 large potatoes, peeled**
½ cup butter	**1 quart heavy cream**
5 sprigs fresh rosemary	**salt and pepper to taste**
¼ cup all-purpose flour	

Wash leeks well and cut white and light-green parts into ¼-inch slices. Slice onion. Melt butter in large frying pan. Sauté onions and leeks 2 to 3 minutes until transparent. Add fresh rosemary. Add flour, blending well. Put onion mixture in large pot with chicken stock. Slice potatoes and add to stock. Simmer until potatoes are cooked. Allow leek and potato soup to cool. Purée in food processor. Add heavy cream, blending well. Season with salt and pepper. Makes approximately 2 quarts.

OLIVE OIL'S ITALIAN RESTAURANT
Aiken

OLIVE OIL'S ITALIAN RESTAURANT

If you arrive at Olive Oil's on a warm spring evening, you might want to find an empty table in the courtyard beside the olive branches, or maybe a cozy one on the front porch. Both locations allow an opportunity to dine alfresco and indulge in a bit of people watching, that popular pastime made famous in the outdoor cafes of Europe.

The colorful yellow cottage with the red, white and green canopy on Chesterfield Street dates back to the 1920s, a time when Aiken was enjoying its heyday. Although the structure was designed as a private residence, destiny had other roles in store. The modest cottage was enlarged through the years, and as it grew it assumed new identities. After a stint as a clothing store, the historic cottage was purchased by imaginative new owners who transformed it into a popular restaurant.

Olive Oil's feels like home the moment you walk in. The restaurant is decidedly cheerful, with its bright rooms usually hosting a simpatico group of people. Original heart-pine floors, an open fireplace and racks filled with imported cans and wine bottles lend just the right touch of informality to the light-hearted bistro atmosphere.

With a name like Olive Oil's, could the restaurant's cuisine be anything but Italian? Expect your mouth to start watering shortly after you arrive, because if the sights and smells of the wonderful Italian dishes here don't start you salivating, the menu will. The favorite appetizer, I was told, is the specialty of the house, Fried Calamari. Following closely are Steamed Mussels or Shrimp and Eggplant Lombardy, a meal in itself featuring marinated shrimp, garlic and tomatoes baked and served over eggplant.

As you might expect, pasta is also a specialty here. You can select your favorite—spinach or egg fettuccine, linguine or angel-hair pasta—and also choose from a selection of delicious homemade sauces. Look for other traditional pasta dishes, too, like Lasagna, Manicotti and Cannelloni, along with an outstanding seafood- and cheese-filled Ravioli prepared with prosciutto ham and a cream sauce that will have you shouting "Bravo!"

People from the Aiken area already know that the creative ideas and deft hands back in the kitchen belong to Bruce Shipman, chef and co-owner. This talented young man often prepares his popular Italian dishes on local television and hosts cooking classes at Olive Oil's on Sundays. His expertise really shines in some of the spectacular entrée selections, like Cioppino, a classic Mediterranean dish of steamed seafood in a saffron-seasoned tomato sauce served over linguine. The wonderful Stuffed Veal with Madeira Sauce is another of his specialties.

The menu matches the easygoing mood at Olive Oil's, with pizza served at lunch and dinner. You might also want to check the wine closet for a good selection of fine Italian wines. If you rèmember to leave room, desserts are prepared fresh every day.

Another inventive crowd-pleaser at Olive Oil's is the monthly Italian recipe contest. Those who submit their favorite Italian recipe have a chance to win a free dinner for two and have their recipe featured as a restaurant special. With such an abundance of creativity bouncing off Olive Oil's high ceilings and walls, it is no wonder this place is winning raves.

Olive Oil's Italian Restaurant is located at 232 Chesterfield Street in Aiken. Lunch is served from 11:30 a.m. until 2:30 p.m., Monday through Friday. Dinner is served from 5:00 p.m. until 11:00 p.m., Monday through Saturday. Reservations are accepted only for parties of eight or more. For information, call (803) 649-3726.

OLIVE OIL'S FRIED CALAMARI

1½ pounds frozen squid (or 3- to 5-inch fresh squid with tentacles)	vegetable cooking oil garlic salt or garlic powder to taste
2 cups flour	cocktail sauce
salt and pepper to taste	lemon

If fresh squid is used, rinse well and remove tentacles and shell. Slice squid. Combine flour and salt and pepper in paper bag and shake to blend. Add squid and shake to coat. Add required amount of oil to deep fryer and fry calamari for 1 to 1½ minutes. Do not overload fryer. Remove squid and drain on paper towels. Season with garlic salt or powder. Serve with cocktail sauce and lemon.

OLIVE OIL'S PASTA ROSE

1 pound pasta
1 red bell pepper, diced
2 teaspoons olive oil
1 box frozen spinach,
    drained and chopped
1½ cups half-and-half
2 cups commercial marinara
    sauce

2 ounces white wine
3 ounces freshly grated
    Parmesan cheese
2 medium tomatoes, diced
salt and pepper to taste

Cook pasta in boiling water to al dente state. Drain and keep warm. Sauté bell pepper in oil until tender. Add spinach, half-and-half, marinara sauce and wine. When mixture is hot, add cheese and tomatoes. Season with salt and pepper and stir until well blended. Pour over warm pasta, toss gently and serve family-style. Serves 4 to 6.

UP YOUR ALLEY
Aiken

UP YOUR ALLEY

Aiken deservedly prides itself on the renovation of the downtown historic area. And in my opinion, there is no place more eye-catching than Up Your Alley. The proprietors of this lively restaurant have innovatively arranged all stools and tables in the saloon so that guests are always at eye level with each other, whether sitting or standing. Psychologically, it is a great icebreaker.

Don't plan to focus your eyes on any one thing for long, however, because the saloon contains quite a collection of memorabilia. Traffic signs, old posters and various license plates, including one from the Cayman Islands, decorate the saloon. I decided to try a drink called "The Alley Cat." This light and frothy drink includes amaretto, pineapple juice and ice cream, and it seemed a perfect way to begin my visit.

Three young men, each with an eye for detail and a pair of deft hands in the kitchen, have cleverly transformed this historic structure into an inviting series of dining rooms. It's hard to believe that the turn-of-the-century building was once considered an eyesore.

The atmosphere in the dining rooms combines Victorian primness with country comfort. Salvaged treasures from old homes and area churches, such as mahogany benches and stained glass, are attractively used throughout. I was particularly impressed with the Music Room, which is decorated with instruments, sheet music and photos of old opera stars.

The food at Up You Alley is every bit as special as the decor. I needed help making a decision and found it when the chef suggested the Fried Artichoke Hearts and Beer Batter Pickles as appetizers. If you have never eaten either of these unusual foods, your taste buds have been living in a state of deprivation.

Since the chef did such a good job with the first course, I left the next one up to him as well. He came through again, because the Avocado Stuffed with Shrimp Salad was a true winner. Other luncheon offerings are such international specialties as pita pocket sandwiches, Tempura-fried Haddock and Mexican burritos.

If you have any room left after finishing the hearty entrées, you may want to choose from the dessert list, which includes such favorites as Cheesecake and fresh fruit. Or you may want to order one of the special liqueur-laced coffees.

Up Your Alley offers an excellent dinner menu that features continental fare like Steak au Poivre, Veal Princess, Scallops Old Saybrook and Chicken Kashmir.

A complete wine list, containing both imported and domestic vintages, is available. The Ulrich Langguth Reisling has become a favorite with local patrons, who consider this quaint restaurant and saloon the "in" place to dine.

Up Your Alley is located at 222 "The Alley" in downtown Aiken. The restaurant is open Monday through Saturday. Lunch is served from 11:30 a.m. until 2:30 p.m. Dinner is served from 5:30 p.m. until 10:00 p.m. Meals are served in the saloon from 11:30 a.m. until 2:00 a.m. For reservations (recommended for dinner), call (803) 649-2603.

UP YOUR ALLEY'S CHICKEN KASHMIR

4 tablespoons clarified butter	2 peach halves
flour	¼ cup mandarin oranges
1 8-ounce boneless chicken breast	1 ounce brandy
	3 ounces Indian chutney
	2 ounces unsalted cashews

Melt butter in a 12-inch sauté pan. Pound chicken breast with meat mallet until flat. Lightly flour chicken breast. Place in pan and sauté for 3 minutes. Turn chicken breast over and sauté on other side for 2 minutes. Add peach halves and mandarin oranges, along with a little of their juices. Reduce this liquid to half and add brandy, chutney and cashews. Serves 1.

UP YOUR ALLEY'S VEAL PRINCESS

2 tablespoons clarified
  butter
8 ounces veal medallions
½ cup all-purpose flour
8 ounces bay scallops

¼ cup sherry
1 cup heavy cream
pinch of tarragon
salt and pepper to taste

Melt butter in a 12-inch sauté pan. Pound veal with a meat mallet until soft. Dredge the medallions in flour and sauté in butter for 1 minute. Turn the veal over and add the scallops. Cook an additional 1 to 2 minutes. Remove veal and scallops from pan and set aside. Add sherry to the skillet to deglaze it. Add cream, tarragon and salt and pepper to pan. Reduce liquid approximately 3 to 5 minutes until creamy. When ready to serve, divide veal and scallops into 4 portions, arranging scallops over medallions. Pour approximately ¼ cup of the cream sauce over each serving. Serves 4.

UP YOUR ALLEY'S "THE ALLEY CAT"

1½ ounces amaretto
2 ounces pineapple juice

3 ounces vanilla ice cream
6 ice cubes

Combine all ingredients in a blender container. Blend on high speed for 1 to 2 minutes. Serve in a brandy snifter. Serves 1.

THE WEST SIDE BOWERY
Aiken

THE WEST SIDE BOWERY

It's hard to believe that the attractive area in downtown Aiken known today as "The Alley" was once a run-down haven for hobos. The district has been handsomely restored and is now one of the city's most popular dining and sightseeing spots.

One of The Alley's main attractions is The West Side Bowery. This restaurant and pub, the area's first renovation project, was the brainchild of Sam Erb. An energetic young man with a dream and lots of help from his family, Erb has made The West Side Bowery a combination of turn-of-the-century charm and today's upbeat atmosphere.

The Bowery, a former stable and carriage house, dates back to the late 1800s. Great care has been taken to preserve and enhance the building. Its original tin ceilings have been reworked, and the handsome hardwood used throughout the restaurant has been rescued from old structures facing demolition. Renovation was a long and difficult process but well worth the effort, as evidenced by the historic preservation award hanging near the entrance.

Creative ideas overflow in this inviting restaurant. On the day that I visited, the building's original exposed-brick walls held the paintings of a local artist's first show. Three paintings had already been sold and it was barely noon. Another "arresting" innovation is the use of a former jail cell, complete with original gates and locks, to display the restaurant's extensive wine collection. The Bowery's decor also acknowledges the fact that horse culture is a way of life for many people in the Aiken area. Lining the walls of the spacious bar are colorful racing silks and photos of Aiken's Derby winners and thoroughbred horse farms. The room is a popular gathering spot for many of the area's elite.

It's a toss-up as to which of the restaurant's dining rooms offers the best view. I chose the bright and cheerful porch, an ideal place to watch action in The Alley. While sipping my iced tea, I could see sightseers browsing in shops and strolling in the miniature "Central Park."

154

The aroma of good food prompted me to turn my attention from the sights to the menu. I was told that The Bowery's Steak Bits, Fried Mushrooms and Potato Skins are favorite appetizers.

For those who prefer seafood, let me suggest the Shrimp Salad Plate. It was almost too pretty to tackle, but I dug in anyway. If you should happen to arrive when Chicken Pretoria is on the menu, you are truly in luck. If not, you will be able to prepare this delicious dish in your own kitchen to the delight of family and friends by following the recipe provided by The Bowery's chef.

There was more action in The Alley that warranted watching, but it was time for me to leave. I promised myself a return to The West Side Bowery during the evening hours, when, I was told, a different but just as pleasing atmosphere awaits.

The West Side Bowery is located at 151 Bee Lane in downtown Aiken. Operating hours are from 11:30 a.m. until 1:00 a.m., Monday through Friday, and from 11:30 a.m. until midnight on Saturday. For reservations (recommended), call (803) 648-2900.

THE WEST SIDE BOWERY'S CHICKEN PRETORIA

Chicken:

6 chicken breasts, skinned and boned	½ cup margarine, melted
salt and pepper to taste	8 ounces finely chopped pecans
3 tablespoons Dijon mustard	3 to 4 tablespoons cooking oil

Preheat oven to 350 degrees. Place chicken between pieces of wax paper and flatten with wooden mallet. Season lightly with salt and pepper. Blend mustard and margarine in medium-sized bowl. Dip chicken into butter mixture, then coat with pecans. Sauté breasts in oil over medium heat until light brown on both sides. Finish by baking in oven about 15 minutes.

Sauce:

1 tablespoon margarine	⅔ cups sour cream
2 tablespoons Dijon mustard	salt and pepper to taste

Melt margarine in pan over low to medium heat. Add sour cream, mustard and salt and pepper. Whisk until well blended and hot. Place tablespoon of sauce on plate and place chicken breast on top. Serves 6.

THE WEST SIDE BOWERY'S BREAD PUDDING

Bread Pudding:

5 ounces stale bread cubes	¼ teaspoon nutmeg
1 cup heavy cream	1 cup milk
4 tablespoons margarine, melted	1 cup sugar
½ cup raisins	1 egg plus 1 egg yolk
1 tablespoon vanilla extract	½ cup chopped pecans
	½ teaspoon cinnamon

Preheat oven to 350 degrees. Combine all ingredients in bowl and blend until mixture is moist. Pour into buttered 3-quart baking dish and bake for 45 minutes.

Vanilla sauce:

½ cup milk	¼ cup granulated sugar
½ cup half-and-half	whipped cream
½ teaspoon vanilla extract	chopped pecans
3 egg yolks	

In a saucepan, scald milk and half-and-half with vanilla. Beat egg yolks and sugar together until thickened and pale in color. Stir into hot milk mixture, blending well. Cook over hot water bath, stirring constantly. Do not boil. Cook until sauce thickens enough to coat a spoon. Strain sauce and let cool. Serve over warm pudding. Top with whipped cream and chopped pecans if desired. Serves 6 to 8.

THE WILLCOX INN
Aiken

THE WILLCOX INN You won't need a historian to tell you that The Willcox Inn is a place with a glorious past. As soon as you lay eyes on the impressive old hotel's sprawling facade, stately columns and handsome balustrade, you'll know that this imposing structure was the epitome of grandeur during Aiken's glittering heyday.

The Willcox Inn was born in 1898 when Englishman Frederick Willcox and his Swedish wife, an excellent cook and caterer, were persuaded to open their gracious home to visitors. It was a success from the start, due in part to the inn's strategic location beside the railroad tracks. This made The Willcox Inn a convenient stop for such distinguished visitors as Winston Churchill, Franklin Delano Roosevelt, the duke of Windsor and some of the great names of America's social set—Mellon, Astor, Barrymore. With all that "royalty" milling about, it comes as no surprise to learn that the distinguished inn later became the American headquarters of the British polo team and the site of Triple Crown after-race parties.

Time eventually took its toll on the grand old sporting hotel, and by the early 1950s The Willcox Inn was boarded up, with one wing burned. There was even talk of condemning the structure. But thanks to the creative foresight and preservationist attitude of a group of Charlestonians, The Willcox Inn escaped the wrecking ball. It was restored and reopened in 1984. Today, the style and grace of a dignified country manor live again at this lovely inn, which offers guest rooms of distinction and an impressive dining room and pub.

The entrance to the dining room is through the luxurious lobby, which contains granite open-hearth fireplaces, original pine paneling and beams, comfortable sofas and a baby grand piano for evening entertainment. You'll discover that the dining room incorporates the same dignified but comfortable atmosphere. Double linens drape the tables, and fresh flowers and sparkling goblets lend a formal air to the traditional setting.

If old Mrs. Willcox were around today, she would surely approve of The Willcox Inn's menu, which offers an interesting selection of highly creative dishes. Because my companion and I were still feeling awed by the elegance of this splendid old structure, we decided to follow the chef's entrée recommendations. We applauded that decision when the Farmhouse Pepper Ducklings arrived. This exquisite dish owes its success to the creamy peppercorn-mustard-brandy sauce that is served with the moist, tender breasts of duckling. Because the dish was well prepared and attractively garnished, we had absolutely no trouble devouring everything on our plates.

Perhaps I could have resisted dessert if anything but the Bread Pudding with Bourbon Sauce and Chantilly Cream had been placed before me. But this sumptuous concoction, richly flavored with spices and nuts and served with a divine butter-bourbon sauce, was so good that I gave in to the temptation.

Another special treat either before or after dinner is a visit to the delightful Polo Pub. This comfortable lounge features an assortment of polo mallets, fly rods and cricket bats and serves as yet another reminder of this historic inn's glorious past.

The Willcox Inn is located at 100 Colleton Avenue at the corner of Whiskey Road in Aiken. Breakfast is served from 7:00 a.m. until 10:00 a.m daily. Lunch is served from 11:30 a.m. until 2:00 p.m., Monday through Friday. Dinner is served from 6:00 p.m. until 9:30 p.m., Monday through Saturday, and from 6:00 p.m. until 8:00 p.m. on Sunday. For reservations (recommended), call (803) 649-1377.

THE WILLCOX INN'S
FARMHOUSE PEPPER DUCKLINGS

4 to 4½ pounds ducklings
salt and pepper to taste
½ cup bottled green
    peppercorns, drained
4 teaspoons Dijon mustard
¼ cup unsalted butter

½ cup brandy
½ cup heavy cream
½ cup thick brown stock
fresh peach halves as an
    accompaniment, if
    desired

Season the ducklings inside and out with salt and pepper and prick the skin all over. In a small bowl, crush ¼ cup of the peppercorns with the mustard. Spread the mixture over the ducklings. Roast the ducklings on a rack in a roasting pan in the middle of a preheated 450-degree oven for 15 minutes. Reduce the heat to 350 degrees and roast 30 minutes more. Transfer the ducklings to a cutting board. When cool, cut into serving pieces, reserving the legs for another use. Heat the butter in a skillet over moderately high heat until the foam subsides. Add duck breasts and sauté for 4 to 5 minutes on each side, until the skin is crisp and the meat is no longer pink. Transfer to a plate. Deglaze the skillet with the brandy, scraping up the brown bits. Add remaining peppercorns, cream, and brown stock. Simmer the sauce, stirring occasionally, for 5 to 6 minutes or until thickened slightly. Season the sauce with salt and pepper. Serve sauce and peach halves with the ducklings. Serves 4.

DENDY CORNER
Abbeville

DENDY CORNER

No, Charles Dendy doesn't live here anymore. Over a century ago, Dendy decided the corner facing Abbeville's town square was no longer a suitable site for his residence, so he moved his home to a more desirable location, leaving behind only his name.

The next structure to rise on the corner vacated by Dendy was the Up Country's first liquor dispensary, built in 1884. Business flourished at the store until Prohibition came along to dampen spirits. A dispensary of another kind moved in during the 1930s, when a filling station opened in the structure. Today, the building houses Dendy Corner, a popular downtown attraction that offers all the ebullience of a neighborhood bar in a relaxed restaurant.

One of the restaurant's most interesting features is the use of split levels. Management informed me that the raised lounge area conceals the former filling station's auto jack. I suppose this lends credence to the old adage that "necessity is the mother of invention."

Other inventive ideas are used throughout this upbeat restaurant. Artfully chipped openings in the plaster walls permit a view of the original brick. Natural-wood latticework partitions separate the bright dining room from the more intimate lounge, where the raised bar overlooks cozy booths. The blend of dark and light wood in the original oak ceiling, sturdy booths and butcher-block tables complements the lustrous wood plank floors.

People watchers can enjoy a table in the front dining room overlooking the action in The Square, with its charming brick-lined streets and Abbeville's historic opera house, now used for contemporary plays. The after-theater crowd can often be found dining at Dendy Corner.

The menu at Dendy Corner is as interesting as the atmosphere. Do-it-yourselfers can dictate the ingredients for their own sandwiches or stuffed potatoes. A variety of quiches, salads and cold plates are also offered.

I had heard about Dendy Corner's Potato Jackets and decided to begin lunch with this appetizer. This is almost a meal in itself, so I shared with friends. They returned the favor and passed along the Nachos and spicy Jalapeño Cheese Dip. Olé to both!

For my entrée, I selected the Cheese Lover's Choice, which is a hefty slice of cheddar atop their ham quiche, and found that it was too good to share. I managed to pass when dessert was offered, although the fresh, sweet concoctions—which vary from day to day—might overwhelm your will power.

Dendy Corner is located on the corner of Pickens Street and South Main on The Square in downtown Abbeville. Meals are served from 11:30 a.m. until 9:45 p.m., Monday through Saturday. For reservations (recommended for dinner), call (803) 459-5800.

DENDY CORNER'S NACHOS

1 16-ounce package
   processed cheese
1 tablespoon mayonnaise
1 4-ounce can chopped
   green chilies

¼ cup minced chives
¼ cup finely diced tomato
Tabasco sauce to taste
½ pound tortilla chips

Cut cheese into small cubes and melt in top of double boiler. Add mayonnaise, chilies, chives and tomato and stir until thoroughly blended. Add Tabasco. Serve warm with tortilla chips for dipping. Yields 2 cups.

DENDY CORNER'S GREAT POTATO HEAD

1 large baking potato
1½ tablespoons butter
1 ounce chopped ham
1 ounce chopped bacon

2 ounces grated cheddar
   cheese
½ cup sour cream

163

Rub potato with 1 teaspoon butter and bake in a 375-degree oven for 1 hour. Slice potato lengthwise and add remaining butter, ham, bacon and cheese. Return to oven and bake at 400 degrees until cheese is melted. Top with sour cream before serving. Serves 1.

DENDY CORNER'S "H.T.B."

3 tablespoons mayonnaise	¼ tablespoon garlic powder
4 tablespoons German mustard	2 slices pumpernickel bread
1 ounce white vinegar	1 ounce ham, thinly sliced
¼ tablespoon curry powder	1 ounce turkey, thinly sliced
1 tablespoon onion salt	1 ounce bacon bits
	2 slices Swiss cheese

Combine mayonnaise, mustard, vinegar, curry powder, onion salt and garlic powder in a small bowl. Mix well to blend flavors. Spread mixture on both slices of pumpernickel. Between bread, layer ham, turkey, bacon bits and cheese. Serves 1.

GRAYSTONE
Laurens

GRAYSTONE

When Graystone was recommended to me as a historic restaurant I should visit, the name immediately conjured up the image of a rustic, old home built of large, gray stones. So strong was this image that I passed right by the restaurant. Graystone didn't resemble my preconceived idea at all.

What I found was an impressive white mansion with stately pillars and a porch that wraps halfway around the building. This grand house was built in the early 1900s for the Gray family, after whom the restaurant is named. It was their home until the early 1960s.

When Tom and Barbara Fischer purchased the mansion in 1968, it was all but hidden behind a thick cover of ivy. As the Fischers began the tedious process of transforming the former residence into a restaurant, it quickly became apparent that they had taken on more of a task than they had anticipâtéd. Even though no major structural changes were required, the renovation process took the family a year of full-time work to complete.

While the Fischers worked at restoring the mansion's lower level, their son Bob—now the manager of the restaurant—and his young friends enjoyed playing in the unoccupied rooms upstairs. One of their favorite rooms was the billiards room, which contained a pool table left behind by the former owners. The youngsters discovered that, along with the pool table, a ghost was left behind—reportedly the spirit of old Mr. Gray. It seems that the gentleman enjoyed the game so much that he returned on certain occasions, after which the boys would discover all the balls mysteriously placed in the pockets. This mischief stopped when the pool table was removed and the billiards room converted into an office.

Upstairs at the restaurant today, you can enjoy an apéritif or an after-dinner nightcap in the comfortable bar and lounge area. You probably won't see a ghost, but you will find a relaxed and dignified atmosphere which echoes that of the dining rooms below.

My table was located beside a bay window in one of the restaurant's most attractive dining rooms. The thick, red carpet created a feeling of warmth, while flickering table candles and hanging baskets of ivy added pleasing touches. The black and white attire worn by waiters and waitresses lent an air of formality.

All of Graystone's signature steaks are aged for up to five weeks, and I daresay you won't find a more tender cut anywhere. The combination plates of beef and seafood are also tempting choices. Those preferring a lighter meal will appreciate the menu selections called "On the Lighter Side." Several seafood selections will satisfy your taste buds and won't overtax your calorie count.

I ordered the Steak and Shrimp, a duo that met my high expectations. I can't rèmember ever having a juicier or more tender cut of meat. I could have cut the petite filet mignon with my fork. Equally tasty were the heap of lightly fried shrimp and the Consommé Rice, a welcome change from the usual potato. A small loaf of freshly baked bread served on a wooden board highlighted my meal.

Graystone is located at 1100 South Harper Street on U.S. 221 South in Laurens. Dinner is served from 5:30 p.m. until 10:00 p.m., Monday through Saturday. For reservations (recommended), call (803) 984-5521.

GRAYSTONE'S SAUTEED STUFFED CHICKEN
IN WHITE WINE

¼ cup sliced mushrooms
1 tablespoon chopped celery
1 tablespoon chopped
   shallots
1 whole chicken breast,
   deboned and skinned

flour
butter for sautéing
½ cup white wine
2 tablespoons cream
3 cherry tomatoes, quartered

Sauté mushrooms, celery and shallots; set aside. Pound chicken very lightly (being sure to leave whole). Place mushroom mixture on half of breast and fold other half over, closing with a toothpick. Very lightly flour both sides. Sauté in butter on both sides. Add wine and cover. Turn once and simmer until done. Remove chicken to towel. Add cream to pan and reduce to desired texture. Add tomatoes. Place chicken on plate and pour sauce over chicken. Serves 1.

GRAYSTONE'S GRAY MAN

1½ ounces Kahlúa
1½ ounces Bailey's Irish
  Cream
½ to ¾ ounce vodka

2 to 3 ounces half-and-half
½ cup crushed ice
3 ounces whipped cream for
  garnish

Pour all ingredients except whipped cream into a blender container. Blend on high speed until well mixed. Pour into 2 brandy snifters. Top each serving with a dollop of whipped cream. Serves 2.

GRAYSTONE'S CONSOMME RICE

1 10-ounce can onion soup
1 10-ounce can beef
  consommé
1 teaspoon butter or
  margarine

½ cup canned, sliced
  mushrooms with liquid
2 cups uncooked converted
  rice

Combine soups and butter in a saucepan. Bring to a boil, then set aside. In a casserole dish, combine mushrooms and rice. Pour soup mixture over rice. Cover and bake in a 350-degree oven for 1 hour. Serves 8.

1109 SOUTH MAIN
Anderson

1109 SOUTH MAIN

They may not be eager to admit it, but Southerners like to picture themselves living in stately antebellum homes where ladies and gentlemen speak in soft voices and gather for dinner in the grand manor. Peter and Myrna Ryter know about this dream. When they opened 1109 South Main in 1982 in the historic Chenault home, their goal was to make the dream possible for their guests. The home was built in 1860 as a wedding present for the daughter of a prominent Anderson family. Today, the setting, the music and the food combine to make visitors feel that they have stepped into a time when life was slower and gentler.

The food at 1109 South Main is continental, with touches of California and the islands thrown in. Three different dining rooms—The Palmetto Room, The Salon and the casual Gauguin Room—set the mood for a memorable dining experience. Guests often wonder about French artist Paul Gauguin's influence on the restaurant. Indeed, who would expect to find the atmosphere of a South Pacific island behind the white columns of an imposing Greek Revival home in Anderson, South Carolina? The answer is that prior to opening 1109 South Main, the Ryters spent four years on the island of Moorea in Tahiti. Many reproductions of Gauguin's paintings of the islands are displayed on the walls. Other treasures garnered during the owners' years in Tahiti include a colorful handmade bedspread and a wall hanging constructed of coconut husks. Any beachcomber will admire the vast collection of seashells.

Impressed as I was with the tropical furnishings, it should come as no surprise that I selected the Hearts of Palm Bora Bora for my salad course. It was everything I hoped it would be— delicious and refreshingly different. Next came the Poisson Cru, an exotic treat of fresh fish chunks marinated in lime juice and coconut milk and served in a coconut shell. I couldn't say no to the Vegetable Mousse, a tasty slice of puréed cauliflower, broccoli and carrots molded into colorful layers, then wrapped in seaweed.

For those not as smitten with island fare, the menu also includes an ample selection of continental and American offerings. Such delicacies as Escargots and Avocado Ambrosia are featured appetizers. Entrées include several choices of seafood and meats. For dessert, a daily selection of tortes, mousses, caramel creams and fresh berries is available. Cocktails and an extensive wine list will also please discriminating diners.

As you would expect, 1109 South Main is located at 1109 South Main Street in Anderson. Dinner is served from 6:00 p.m. until 10:30 p.m., Tuesday through Saturday. The restaurant also serves Easter Sunday brunch and a Christmas Eve buffet. For reservations, call (803) 225-1109.

1109 SOUTH MAIN'S POISSON CRU

2 pounds fresh tuna, swordfish, wahoo or grouper, deboned	1 finely chopped garlic clove
8 limes	dash of salt
2 chopped tomatoes	dash of pepper
1 grated carrot	dash of hot pepper sauce
1 chopped onion	1 pint coconut milk
	lettuce leaves for garnish

Cut fish into 1 × ½-inch pieces. Place fish pieces in a stainless steel or glass bowl and squeeze lime juice over them. Allow fish to marinate in juice for 10 minutes. Pour off the juice, draining well. Add vegetables, garlic, salt, pepper, hot pepper sauce and coconut milk. Mix well with a spoon and serve on lettuce. Serves 4.

Note: Slices of hard-boiled egg and cucumber may be added, if desired.

1109 SOUTH MAIN'S ONION SOUP

4 onions
2 tablespoons cooking oil
1 bay leaf
dash of monosodium
  glutamate
dash of white pepper
½ teaspoon Worcestershire
  sauce

1 cup white wine
1 quart chicken broth or
  bouillon
4 to 6 slices bread
1 cup grated Swiss cheese

Peel onions; cut in half and finely slice. In a soup pan, heat oil. Add onions and sauté until tender. Add bay leaf, monosodium glutamate, pepper and Worcestershire sauce; cook ingredients until onions are golden brown. Add wine and chicken broth and cook over medium heat for 10 minutes. Pour soup into individual ovenproof serving bowls and top each with a bread slice and 2 tablespoons of grated cheese. Place bowls under broiler until cheese is melted. Serves 4 to 6.

Note: The soup may be kept for days in the refrigerator and may be reheated before serving.

THE MORRIS STREET TEA ROOM
Anderson

THE MORRIS STREET TEA ROOM

When you visit The Morris Street Tea Room, be sure to watch for the ghosts carrying pink umbrellas and dancing about the grounds. Legend has it that these playful spirits are the deceased members of the eccentric Morris family, which occupied the distinguished-looking structure in the late 1800s.

The Morrises were transplanted from sophisticated Charleston society to what they considered "common" Anderson. Perhaps the dance with pink umbrellas was a fashionable number performed by Charleston high society of the day. I would have loved to see the ghosts, but no such colorful sight appeared. Nevertheless, my disappointment faded as soon as I entered the old mansion and found a dining room decorated in the loveliest shades of—you guessed it—pink.

Pink is not the only color you'll find inside the restored house. You're bound to come across your favorite color combination in one of the four dining rooms, each named after one of the mansion's former owners. The Caldwell Room, with its pale pink walls and rose-colored tablecloths, seemed the most romantic. But I didn't mind being led to the cinnamon-hued Johnson Room, which gets its name from the original owner, who also founded Anderson's first female academy.

Heavenly smells drifted from the kitchen, where owner Angie Finazzo carefully prepares her culinary masterpieces. Some of the most requested items on the luncheon menu are the quiches. After one bite of the petite Mademoiselles Quiche, a delicious blend of cheeses, eggs, cream, shrimp and crab, I understood why the Finazzos are constantly badgered to market the item. One of the ingredients that makes this dish so special is the cream cheese used in the pastry crust.

The restaurant's dinner menu offers such enticing continental choices as Veal Medallions and Duck à l'Orange. An extensive wine list includes both imported and domestic wines, as well as unusual beers and ales.

I made a note to return on a Sunday, when an abundant buffet offers a variety of dishes. Each week, a different country's cuisine is featured alongside the restaurant's regular offerings. Such a tempting array of good food will undermine the most dedicated dieter, so try to leave the calorie counter at home. However, if dieting is uppermost on your mind, then plan to choose from several salads that always appear on the menu and on the Sunday buffet.

The Morris Street Tea Room is located at 220 East Morris Street in Anderson. Lunch is served from 11:00 a.m. until 2:00 p.m., Tuesday through Saturday. Sunday buffet is served from 11:00 a.m. until 2:00 p.m. Dinner is served from 6:00 p.m. until 9:00 p.m., Monday through Saturday, but on a reservations-only basis on Monday, Tuesday and Wednesday. Reservations for the other nights are preferred but not required. The phone number is (803) 226-7307.

THE MORRIS STREET TEA ROOM'S
CHICKEN SOUP FLORENTINE

1 bunch fresh spinach
2 quarts chicken broth
4 ounces tiny, thin egg
   noodles, cooked

Parmesan cheese for garnish
grated carrots for garnish

Cut raw spinach into fine strips and place in serving bowls. Heat chicken broth until hot. Add pasta to broth just before serving. Pour broth mixture over spinach and lace with Parmesan cheese. Garnish with grated carrots. Serves 6.

THE MORRIS STREET TEA ROOM'S
QUICHE ANGIE

3 ounces soft cream cheese
½ cup soft butter
1 cup flour
6 slices bacon
1½ cups heavy cream

2 eggs plus 2 egg yolks
½ teaspoon salt
pinch of white pepper
¾ cup grated Swiss cheese
2 tablespoons cubed butter

Prepare quiche crust by combining cream cheese, ½ cup butter and flour with an electric mixer. Remove dough from mixer bowl and knead into the shape of a ball; wrap with protective cloth and refrigerate. While pastry dough is chilling, cook and chop the bacon and set it aside. Blend cream, eggs, salt and pepper with electric mixer until blended. Roll out or pat chilled dough into an 8-inch or 9-inch quiche pan. Add Swiss cheese and bacon pieces; pour egg mixture over all. Place butter cubes on top. Bake at 375 degrees for 30 to 45 minutes until quiche is puffed and firm and a knife inserted in the center comes out clean. Serves 4 to 6.

THE MORRIS STREET TEA ROOM'S
ITALIAN CREAM PIE

1 deep 9-inch pie shell
1 quart half-and-half
4 cinnamon sticks
1 cup sugar
2 teaspoons vanilla
1 5⅓-ounce can evaporated
    milk

¾ cup cornstarch
1 cup heavy cream, whipped
1 square of unsweetened
    chocolate for garnish

Bake the pie shell and let it cool. Heat half-and-half with cinnamon sticks in a saucepan until hot; do not boil. Remove cinnamon sticks and reduce heat to simmer. Add sugar and vanilla to the mixture. Blend evaporated milk and cornstarch together until smooth. Add to warm mixture and stir until thick. Pour into the pie shell and chill until set. Top with whipped cream. Shave chocolate curls and garnish as desired. Yields 1 pie.

FARMERS HALL RESTAURANT
Pendleton

FARMERS HALL RESTAURANT

I t's easy to mistake Farmers Hall Restaurant for the official-looking courthouse it was originally designed to be back in the 1820s. No other building on my historic restaurants list looks less like an eating establishment. Situated on the village green in downtown Pendleton, the towering white structure with enormous concrete columns flanking the back and front doors is the oldest farmers' hall in existence today.

It was no small feat, transforming the austere concrete building's lower level into a warm and inviting restaurant, but a good dose of creativity and imagination did just that. Soft watercolor paintings are displayed on the cheerful, floral-papered walls, while old-timey lace curtains soften the peach-pink shutters. Like many old buildings, Farmers Hall is graced with nooks and crannies—one cranny is used to display delicate antique china, while another nook is large enough for a private dining alcove.

The Pendleton Farmers Society purchased the stately structure over 150 years ago, after district changes altered the need for the courthouse. Its members still meet upstairs, no doubt after stopping below for some tasty victuals.

I arrived at Farmers Hall in time for lunch and had no trouble whatsoever making a decision. When white, shell-shaped dishes overflowing with Chicken Salad arrived at a table across the room, I knew I had to have the same. I made the right choice, because the salad tasted as good as it looked. The combination of chicken chunks, pineapple, raisins and pecans was only surpassed by the melt-in-your-mouth Sour Cream Biscuits that have earned Farmers Hall a reputation. I also sampled a bit of the delicious Seafood au Gratin, which has a wonderfully fresh, tangy quality. But the surprise of the day was the innovative Chicken Reuben. One bite and I knew I had to have the recipe. A man at the next table told me I shouldn't leave out the Meat Pie, so I tried that hearty combination as well.

The desserts at Farmers Hall reminded me of a church social. With all I'd eaten already, you would have thought I couldn't pack in one more bite. Wrong! Who can pass up Lemonade

178

Chiffon or Sour Cream Coconut Pie? I certainly couldn't. I would have tried the Hummingbird Cake, too, but the man who suggested trying the Meat Pie was contentedly sighing over their last piece.

Farmers Hall Restaurant is located on The Square in Pendleton. Lunch is served from 11:00 a.m. until 2:30 p.m., Tuesday through Saturday. Dinner is served from 5:00 p.m. until 10:00 p.m. on Friday and Saturday. For reservations (preferred), call (803) 646-7024.

FARMERS HALL RESTAURANT'S
CHICKEN SALAD

1½ cups cooked chicken
½ cup boiling water
¼ cup white raisins
½ cup crushed pineapple
3 scallions, finely chopped
½ cup chopped celery

¼ cup broken pecans
½ cup mayonnaise
1 teaspoon dried tarragon
1 teaspoon salt
¼ teaspoon white pepper
fresh parsley

Tear chicken into bite-sized pieces. Pour boiling water over raisins and let stand for 5 minutes. Drain. Add raisins, pineapple, scallions, celery and pecans to chicken. In a separate bowl, combine mayonnaise, tarragon, salt and white pepper. Add to chicken mixture, stirring until thoroughly mixed. Garnish with parsley. Serves 4.

FARMERS HALL RESTAURANT'S
CHICKEN REUBEN

4 deboned and skinned
   chicken breasts
⅓ cup all-purpose flour
4 tablespoons margarine

4 tablespoons Thousand
   Island dressing
4 tablespoons sauerkraut
4 slices Swiss cheese

Flatten chicken with a meat mallet. Dust both sides with flour. Melt margarine in a skillet and sauté chicken on both sides until brown. Remove from skillet and spread 1 tablespoon of dressing on each chicken breast. Spread 1 tablespoon of sauerkraut evenly over each chicken breast. Top each with a slice of Swiss cheese. Place on a greased baking sheet and bake in a preheated 375-degree oven for 20 minutes. Serves 4.

FARMERS HALL RESTAURANT'S
SEAFOOD AU GRATIN

1 cup imitation crabmeat
1 cup small shrimp, cleaned
¾ cup mild cheddar cheese, shredded
2 to 3 scallions, finely chopped

½ cup mayonnaise
½ cup whipping cream
⅓ cup Parmesan cheese
⅓ cup breadcrumbs
⅓ cup chopped parsley

Put crabmeat and shrimp in a medium-sized bowl. Add cheddar, scallions and mayonnaise. Mix to combine. Put mixture into a greased 1½-quart casserole. Pour unwhipped whipping cream over mixture. Combine Parmesan, breadcrumbs and parsley and sprinkle evenly over top. Bake in a preheated 375-degree oven for 15 minutes or until bubbly. Serves 4 to 6.

FARMERS HALL RESTAURANT'S
SOUR CREAM BISCUITS

2 cups self-rising flour
4 tablespoons shortening

⅔ cup sour cream
½ to ¾ cup milk

Combine flour, shortening and sour cream. Add milk until mixture is of spooning consistency. Drop by the tablespoonful onto a greased pan. Bake in a 450-degree oven for 8 to 10 minutes. Serve immediately. Yields 2 dozen biscuits.

Note: Biscuits are also good rewarmed.

LIBERTY HALL INN
Pendleton

LIBERTY HALL INN **W**hile scouting restaurants in Pendleton, I passed Liberty Hall Inn twice, each time looking back wistfully at the old Southern-style Piedmont Plantation architecture. My curiosity finally got the better of me, and I backtracked to its circular driveway.

Once inside, I learned that the house had only five large rooms plus a detached kitchen when Thomas and Nancy Sloan built it in the 1840s as a retreat from the heat and disease of Charleston summers. The home was later sold to W. B. Hall.

In 1890, Bonneau Harris, South Carolina's commissioner of agriculture and the manager of nearby Woodburn Plantation, purchased the home for his growing family. He more than doubled the size of the house and the acreage that went with it. He also attached the same kitchen that is in use today. His wife ran the home as a boardinghouse and was noted for her good meals. During the family's fifty-year tenure, male teenage relatives of the Harrises were sent to "Harris Hall" for the summer to work with the sheep, in the dairy or in the orchard to keep them out of mischief. That system worked well until 1933, when fresh hay stored in the barn caught fire. The roaring fire that burned the barn would have consumed the house as well, if not for a fire hydrant that had been installed on the property that same week. Thank goodness that providence, or town planners, intervened!

The 1985 restoration of Liberty Hall Inn could be a picture in a history book. What I like best about the restoration is its authenticity. Thankfully, air conditioning and private baths have been added to the inn's ten bedrooms, but they haven't altered the sense that one has stepped into a place straight out of the late 1800s.

Of the two dining rooms, I chose the peach-colored, airy one opening onto the deck. My four-course meal began with soup du jour. That evening's offering, Cream of Asparagus served with warm French rolls and butter, was rich and appetite-awakening. This course was followed by a crisp and tangy salad served with the inn's own creamy Poppy Seed Dressing. Two of the six main courses that night were variations on Orange Roughy. I sampled both and slightly preferred the Orange Roughy Parmesan over the Mediterranean offering. Beef enthusiasts will love the Marinated Beef Tenderloin, which my husband heartily endorsed. I've eaten crab cakes up and down the coast, but never have I had any that contained more crab per cake than those delicately seasoned ones at Liberty Hall. That evening, they also served Lemon-garlic Chicken, which is easy on the calories and cholesterol but does not forsake taste. One of their nicest offerings is Veal Lombardy, a blend of local pasture-raised veal sautéed in mushrooms and white wine. The inn also has a remarkable wine list you can enjoy without having to take out a loan.

I knew I had sinned enough for one day, so I said no to the Chocolate Sin dessert. But that won't be the case the next time I visit this wonderful restaurant and inn, where I plan to spend a night or maybe even a weekend.

Liberty Hall Inn is located at 621 South Mechanic Street in Pendleton. Dinner is served from 6:00 p.m. until 9:00 p.m., Monday through Saturday. Private luncheons are available by arrangement. For reservations (appreciated), call (803) 646-7500.

LIBERTY HALL'S ORANGE ROUGHY PARMESAN

1 8-ounce package herb-
   seasoned stuffing mix
½ cup grated Parmesan
   cheese
1 tablespoon garlic salt

1 bunch parsley, chopped
4 6-ounce orange roughy
   filets
kiwi slices or lemon wedges

Combine stuffing mix with cheese, garlic salt and parsley in a medium-sized bowl until well mixed. Roll filets in breading mix and place in a greased shallow baking pan. Bake in a preheated 375-degree oven for 15 to 20 minutes or until done. Garnish with kiwi slices or lemon wedges. Serves 4.

LIBERTY HALL'S MARINATED BEEF TENDERLOIN

½ cup ruby port wine
¼ cup olive oil
¼ cup soy sauce
½ teaspoon hot-pepper
  sauce

1 bay leaf
½ teaspoon dried thyme
2 pounds boneless beef-
  tenderloin steaks, ½-inch
  thick

Combine all ingredients except beef in a large nonreactive container (ceramic or plastic). Stir until incorporated. Cut meat into 4 steaks. Add steaks to marinade. Cover and refrigerate for 3 to 6 hours, turning occasionally. (Longer marinating may alter texture of meat.) In preheated 450-degree oven, heat wire racks inside foil-lined baking pans for 5 to 10 minutes. Place steaks on wire racks and bake for 7 minutes. Turn and bake 7 minutes more. Cook until steaks register 130 degrees (medium rare) on a meat thermometer. Serves 4.

LIBERTY HALL'S LEMON-GARLIC CHICKEN

4 8-ounce chicken breasts,
  deboned and skinned
seasoned flour for dredging
4 tablespoons butter
1 teaspoon garlic, minced

1 tablespoon lemon juice
ground pepper to taste
⅓ cup white wine
lemon wedges and parsley
  for garnish

Dust chicken on both sides with flour. Melt butter in sauté pan. Stir in garlic, lemon juice and pepper. Sauté chicken on both sides until light brown. Place chicken in a greased baking pan. Deglaze sauté pan with wine; pour over chicken. Bake in a preheated 375-degree oven for 20 to 25 minutes, or until chicken is cooked through. Garnish with lemon wedges and parsley. Serves 4.

PENDLETON HOUSE
RESTAURANT AND PUB
Pendleton

PENDLETON HOUSE The architecture of East Main Street in Pendleton is Southern to the core, and no building more strikingly so than Pendleton House, with its covered front porch that stretches the entire width of the home. This 1880 house doesn't look awfully large from the street, but the exterior appearance is deceptive. Once you're inside, the size is overwhelming. You could do a lively two-step on the heart-pine floors that extend through the rustic foyer. The walls are the original wide pine, and owner Jinny Morgan says she'd be run out of town if she wallpapered them.

Pendleton Pub is an inviting first stop whether you'd like to play a game of darts or just sit beside the fireplace in one of their church pews. I must say that sitting in a church pew sipping a before-dinner drink had a devilish appeal for me. You can also play backgammon, or listen to local people who often drop by with their guitars, or go into the adjoining Drawing Room to unwind on soft sofas and listen to Jinny's oral menu. Her goal is to get a chuckle from each customer. Her patter runs something like this: "Tonight, we're serving Pan-broiled Lamb Tenderloin. You can have that with Mint Jelly because it's traditional, with Hot Pepper Jelly because we're Southern, or with Chutney because this is a classy joint."

Jinny encourages guests to have their appetizers in the Drawing Room, but since I ordered Crab Bisque, I crossed the grand dining room with its beautiful chandeliers to a small dining room on the other side of the house. I've had many good bisques before, but never one with Pendleton House's innovative combination of crab and asparagus. It was a worthwhile marriage of flavors. I was intrigued by their "Salmon" Trout, which Jinny identified as a trout with an identity crisis, but I chose the Shrimp Mediterranean instead. The taste proved to be as colorful as the name, offering a spicy blend of tomatoes and garlic over linguini.

I sampled not one but two desserts. The luscious Chocolate Truffle Loaf with Raspberry Sauce reminded me of the richness of European chocolate combined with the tartness of raspberries. But I had to have the Bristol Cream Sherry Cake, a recipe passed down from Jinny's mother. It is very rich and very, very sinful, but who thinks about abstaining when you're dining in such a classy joint?

Pendleton House Restaurant and Pub is located at 203 East Main Street in Pendleton. Dinner is served from 5:00 p.m. until 11:00 p.m., Tuesday through Saturday. For reservations, call (803) 646-7795.

PENDLETON HOUSE'S
BRISTOL CREAM SHERRY CAKE

Cake:

4 large eggs	1 box yellow cake mix
¾ cup vegetable oil	1 small package instant
¾ cup Harvey's Bristol	lemon pudding
Cream Sherry	½ teaspoon nutmeg

Beat eggs, oil and sherry with an electric mixer until frothy. Sift together cake mix, pudding and nutmeg. Add gradually to egg mixture. Beat on low speed until blended. Beat on medium speed until smooth. Pour into a greased and floured bundt or tube pan. Bake at 350 degrees for approximately 45 minutes. Let cool on rack for 20 minutes. Turn out on a serving plate.

Glaze:

⅔ cup sugar	1 to 2 tablespoons brandy
½ cup water	

Boil sugar and water for 3 to 4 minutes. Remove from heat and stir in brandy. Pierce cake intermittently with a fork. Pat on glaze with a pastry brush, thoroughly coating cake and allowing glaze to soak in.

187

Garnish:

1 cup heavy whipping
   cream
1 tablespoon sugar

nutmeg
red seedless grapes
green seedless grapes

Whip cream with sugar. Cut cake into slices and garnish each slice with a generous dollop of whipped cream. Sprinkle with nutmeg and decorate with grapes. Yields 1 cake.

PENDLETON HOUSE'S
SHRIMP MEDITERRANEAN

1 8-ounce package linguini
1 teaspoon chopped parsley
garlic salt to taste
1 to 2 tablespoons butter
1 tablespoon olive oil
½ yellow onion, julienned
   very thin
3 to 4 cloves garlic, diced
1 large tomato, diced
24 large shrimp, peeled and
   deveined

6 medium-sized fresh
   mushrooms, sliced
2 teaspoons dried rosemary
2 teaspoons dried cilantro
1 teaspoon lemon juice
4 tablespoons unsalted
   butter
1 8-ounce can artichoke
   hearts, drained and
   quartered
parsley for garnish

Prepare linguini according to package directions. Add parsley, garlic salt and 1 to 2 tablespoons butter to drained linguini. Toss to coat evenly. Set aside and keep warm. Heat olive oil in a large cast-iron skillet or sauté pan. Add onion and garlic and sauté for 1 minute. Add tomato and sauté for 1 minute. Add shrimp and cook about 1 minute until al dente. Add mushrooms, rosemary and cilantro. Add lemon juice and toss to distribute herbs evenly, cooking about 1 minute more. Reduce heat and add 4 tablespoons unsalted butter and artichokes. Taste and add salt if needed. When butter is melted but not oily, toss and serve over pasta. Garnish with parsley. Serves 4.

CALHOUN CORNERS RESTAURANT
Clemson

CALHOUN CORNERS RESTAURANT

Back in the early 1800s, before Clemson was an educational center, it was undisputedly "Calhoun Country." Some 814 acres of rolling hills make up Fort Hill, the estate of South Carolina's most illustrious statesman, John C. Calhoun. This fiery orator persuaded Congress to declare war on Britain in 1812 and continued to fight against tyranny until his death.

The senator's staunch defense of states' rights endeared him to Carolinians, who felt the oppression of high tariffs until Calhoun worked out a compromise in 1832. So strong, in fact, was the love for this colorful senator that even today Calhoun Corners Restaurant retains his name. Originally, the whole area was called Calhoun. But after Thomas Clemson, John Calhoun's son-in-law, donated land for an agricultural university, it became known as Clemson. Today, Calhoun's Fort Hill mansion is the focal point of Clemson University.

When the structure that houses Calhoun Corners Restaurant was built in 1893, it was constructed of handmade brick and was designed to be used as a social center for the community. After a few years, however, it became the home of Fort Hill Presbyterian Church for an interim period. When the church relocated, the building was converted into a general store. Today, it is again a social center, as many consider this delightful restaurant the "in" place to dine in Clemson.

When the historic structure changed hands in 1974, there was no need for major structural alterations. The brick walls, wooden plank floors and lofty ceiling beams probably look much the same as they did at the turn of the century. The current decor reflects a comfortable, country atmosphere, with its interesting assortment of Ansel Adams prints, country scenes and antique mirrors.

The kitchen at Calhoun Corners has a reputation for preparing the most wonderful prime ribs of beef. While the restaurant takes particular pride in its tender cuts of steak, visitors will also be happy to find fresh seafood and fowl entrées on the menu.

Take my word for it, the excellent Seafood Fettucini could make a believer out of any dedicated meat eater.

Lunch at Calhoun Corners mainly features sandwiches. The hottest-selling items in the sandwich department are the Hot Vegetarian Sandwich, the Seafood Melt and the Chicken Cordon Bleu Sandwich. The staff advised me that soups are also popular. I enjoyed a steaming bowl of Rosy Onion Soup, spiced with oregano to give it a special zip.

Calhoun Corners Restaurant is located at 103 Clemson Street in Clemson. Lunch is served from 11:30 a.m. until 1:45 p.m., Monday through Friday. Dinner is served from 5:00 p.m. until 10:00 p.m., Monday through Saturday. For reservations (recommended for dinner), call (803) 654-7490.

CALHOUN CORNERS RESTAURANT'S
SEAFOOD FETTUCINI

4 teaspoons butter
½ clove garlic, minced
1 teaspoon shallots, finely
   diced
½ pound bay scallops
6 ounces crabmeat
12 to 14 medium shrimp,
   cleaned

¼ cup white wine
1 cup heavy cream
½ cup grated Parmesan
   cheese
salt and pepper to taste
½ pound cooked fettucini

Melt butter in a skillet over medium heat and sauté garlic and shallots until translucent. Add scallops, crabmeat and shrimp. Sauté 2 to 3 minutes until tender. Remove mixture from skillet and keep warm. Drain skillet and deglaze with wine. Add cream and cheese. Reduce heat, stirring frequently to keep mixture from sticking. Season with salt and pepper. Pour seafood over fettucini and top with sauce. Serves 4.

CALHOUN CORNERS RESTAURANT'S
POTATO CELERY SOUP

5 medium potatoes, peeled
 and diced
5 medium onions, diced
4 cups chicken broth
6 stalks celery, diced

1 tablespoon butter
2 cups sour cream
2 cups half-and-half
salt and pepper to taste

In a soup pot, cook potatoes and onions in chicken broth until barely tender. Add celery and continue to cook until completely tender. Partially mash the potatoes and add butter. In a separate bowl, combine 2 cups of the soup mixture with the sour cream. Whip with a whisk until thoroughly blended and smooth. Pour into soup. Add half-and-half; stir over low heat. Do not boil after sour cream and half-and-half are added. Season with salt and pepper. Serves 6 to 8.

CALHOUN CORNERS RESTAURANT'S
ROSY ONION SOUP

1½ tablespoons butter
4 large onions, diced
2 cups water
1 10-ounce can chicken
 broth
1 teaspoon oregano

¼ cup sugar
1 10-ounce can diced
 tomatoes
1 cup tomato purée
dash of Tabasco sauce
dash of salt and pepper

Melt butter in a soup pot. Add onions and sauté until tender. Add the remaining ingredients. Simmer for 2 to 3 hours. Serves 4.

SEVEN OAKS
Greenville

SEVEN OAKS

The quality of workmanship in the stately mansion surrounded by towering oak trees on Broadus Avenue will most likely never be seen again. But the million-dollar restoration of the circa-1895 structure was worth the effort.

Upon entering the gleaming white mansion with the sweeping wraparound porch, I understood why Seven Oaks is considered Greenville's premier restaurant. The first word that came to mind was Posh, spelled with a capital P. Seven Oaks must be seen to be believed. From the tastefully furnished entrance hall and dining rooms, with their antique chandeliers and sconces, to the polished woodwork and handsome, original rock-maple floors, the transformation has been a gratifying success.

The interplay of colors used throughout the six dining rooms and two lounges can only be described as fascinating. Shades of brown, rose, burgundy and peach flow together in consistent harmony, yet each room is allowed a distinctive decor. Waiters in tuxedos quietly glide about to the soft strains of classical music.

I was seated upstairs in a sophisticated dining room decorated with burgundy-colored walls and creamy lace draperies that gave the room a sublime richness. But let me assure you, the dramatic colors weren't the only impressive features. Making a dining decision with a menu listing such irresistible items as Beef Wellington, Garlic Steak, Pecan Chicken and New Zealand Green Lip Mussels and Pasta proved to be quite an undertaking.

Since the restaurant's reputation for Cream of Shiitake Mushroom Soup is well known, I began with this velvety soup underscored with a subtle nutty flavor. I found that it exceeded even my high expectations. Because I'm partial to appetizers, I also sampled their Scallops and Mushrooms. This is an interesting combination of scallops accented with the unique flavors of shimeji mushrooms and bleu cheese. Most people would not order two dishes with mushrooms, but these mushrooms were dissimilar enough to risk the choice. With six steak entrées on the menu, I took the hint and tried the Garlic Steak prepared in elephant garlic oil. This is an unusual twist on the standard filet mignon.

Calorie counting took a backseat when the dessert cart arrived. I'm glad my attitude was so relaxed, because it allowed me to sample two tasty desserts. The Vienna Raspberry Cream Roll combined layers of raspberries and butter-cream pudding rolled up in a sponge cake, then decorated with strawberries and chocolate. It fit the definition of decadent desserts, being both filling and fantastic. But the homemade Tollhouse Cookies, served hot in a six-inch skillet and topped with ice cream and chocolate sauce, were equally wicked.

I rounded out my meal with a decaf cappuccino, which permitted me the time to reflect upon the era of the mansion's construction, when perfection was a nonnegotiable item. I quickly realized that the ambiance at Seven Oaks achieves that same goal today.

Seven Oaks is located at 104 Broadus Avenue in Greenville. Dinner is served from 6:00 p.m. until 10:00 p.m., Monday through Saturday. Luncheons are available through special arrangements. For reservations, call (803) 232-1895.

SEVEN OAKS'
VIENNA RASPBERRY CREAM ROLL

1 1.4-ounce package vanilla pudding mix
4 large eggs
1 cup sugar
1 cup all-purpose flour, sifted
additional sugar for sprinkling

1 cup butter, softened
1 teaspoon rum extract
1 10-ounce can raspberry pie filling
4 ounces European semisweet chocolate
12 fresh strawberries

Prepare pudding according to package directions and refrigerate. Combine eggs and sugar and beat with an electric mixer for 6 to 8 minutes until mixture masses in volume and is pale

195

yellow. Sift flour over egg mixture a little at a time; fold in gently but thoroughly. Cut a piece of parchment or wax paper to fit inside a jelly-roll pan (15 × 10 ×1). Brush paper thoroughly with cooking oil, including sides of pan. Pour cake mixture into pan and bake in a 425-degree oven for 10 to 12 minutes until golden brown. (Cake should spring back to the touch.) Moisten a paper towel and sprinkle sugar over it. Turn out cake onto towel. Sprinkle sugar on other side of cake and roll cake up gently. Let cool. Mix softened butter with an electric mixer until pliable. Add pudding by tablespoons until well blended. Add rum extract and mix until combined. Roll out cake; remove towel. Spread a layer of pudding mixture over cake. Spread raspberry filling over pudding mixture and roll cake up again. Spread remaining pudding mixture over cake. Shave chocolate into curls and garnish cake with chocolate and strawberries. Yields 1 cake.

SEVEN OAKS' SCALLOPS AND MUSHROOMS

4 ounces sea scallops
2 ounces shimeji
  mushrooms
2 ounces white wine
1 ounce bleu cheese,
  crumbled
2 ounces heavy whipping
  cream

salt and white pepper to
  taste
2 4-inch commercial pastry
  puffs, baked according to
  package directions
parsley

Sauté scallops and mushrooms with wine 2 to 3 minutes until scallops are done. Add bleu cheese, stirring to melt. Reduce heat and pour in whipping cream. Cook 1 minute but do not allow to boil. Season with salt and white pepper. Remove tops of warm pastry puffs and ladle mixture inside. Replace tops and sprinkle with parsley. Serves 2.

THE PIAZZA TEA ROOM
Spartanburg

THE PIAZZA TEA ROOM

There is an enchanted place where summer lasts all year. It is a sparkling white porch where ferns burst through hanging baskets and sunlight streams through high, arched windows. Although I was told that this serene back porch is irresistible during the spring when the dogwoods are in bloom, it couldn't have been more pleasing on the winter day of my visit.

I often hoped to find a special place where I could take my Yankee friends when I want to show them what Southern grace and hospitality are all about. There is no need to look any longer, because as soon as I stepped into The Piazza Tea Room, I knew the search was over.

The historic structure that houses the tea room dates back to 1909. It has played many roles in Spartanburg's history. Local residents remember when the grand old home was a dormitory for students attending Converse College, located across the street. But the most prominent memories are of the many times the home was used as a Halloween haunted house. Needless to say, ghosts and goblins would not be able to recognize the renovated building today.

The food served at The Piazza Tea Room is truly special. Each dish on the menu is explained in mouth-watering detail, so don't be surprised if you want to order everything listed. The Salmagundi, an eighteenth-century name for a chef's salad, is a meal in itself. You'll also find soups, sandwiches, hot entrées and combination plates.

Because I was in the mood for sampling a variety of goodies, I ordered the Tea Sandwich Platter, a house specialty. It's obvious why this selection is so popular—it's a culinary work of art. I didn't want to make a dent in the Frozen Date Soufflé, which was surrounded by petite tea sandwiches and fresh fruit, but after the first bite I forgot about art and attended to appetite.

Instead of wine or coffee, I chose a pot of Hot Spiced Tea to complement my meal. This full-bodied brew was so good I asked for the recipe. If you have never had the pleasure of enjoying tea prepared this way, do yourself a favor and make it.

The tea room's grand finale is an incredible selection of homemade desserts. You won't find run-of-the-mill desserts here. There are pies with unusual names—Mud, Fox Head and Brownie, for instance—and cheesecakes flavored with chocolate chips, pralines or amaretto. I chose the Sawdust Pie, filled with pecans and coconut and topped with whipped cream, banana slices and a maraschino cherry.

The Piazza Tea Room is located in Galleria on Main on the corner of East Main Street and Mills Avenue in Spartanburg. Lunch is served from 11:30 a.m. until 2:00 p.m., Monday through Saturday. Beverages and desserts are served from 11:30 a.m. until 5:00 p.m., Monday through Friday. For reservations (preferred), call (803) 585-0606.

THE PIAZZA TEA ROOM'S SAWDUST PIE

1½ cups sugar	1 unbaked 9-inch pie shell
1½ cups flaked coconut	1 cup whipped cream
1½ cups chopped pecans	1 sliced banana
1½ cups graham-cracker crumbs	maraschino cherries for garnish
7 egg whites	

Preheat oven to 350 degrees. Combine sugar, coconut, pecans and graham-cracker crumbs in a medium bowl. Add unbeaten egg whites and blend with a spoon until thoroughly mixed, but do not beat. Pour into the pie shell. Bake until filling is set, about 30 to 35 minutes. Serve warm or at room temperature. Top each serving with a dollop of whipped cream, a few banana slices and a stemmed cherry. Yields 1 pie.

THE PIAZZA TEA ROOM'S
FROZEN DATE SOUFFLE

1 8-ounce package cream
  cheese

¼ cup maple syrup

2 medium-sized ripe
  bananas

1 tablespoon lemon juice

1 8-ounce can crushed
  pineapple, drained

½ cup finely chopped dates

½ cup finely chopped
  pecans

1 cup whipping cream

Allow cream cheese to soften and place it in a medium bowl. Beat syrup into cheese with an electric mixer. Mash the bananas and combine them with lemon juice; add to cream cheese and beat until thoroughly blended. Stir in pineapple, dates and pecans. Whip the cream and fold it into the soufflé mixture. Gently stir until well blended. Spoon into paper-lined muffin tins and freeze until firm. Allow to soften slightly before serving. Serves 12.

THE PIAZZA TEA ROOM'S HOT SPICED TEA

1 12-ounce can frozen
  lemonade

1 6-ounce can frozen orange
  juice

1 12-ounce can pineapple
  juice

4 quarts boiling water

5 family-size tea bags

1¼ cups sugar

2 teaspoons whole allspice

lemon slices for garnish

1 teaspoon whole cloves

Allow juices to thaw. Add boiling water to tea bags; cover and steep for 10 minutes. Pour tea into a 30-cup electric percolator. Add juices and sugar. Place allspice in the basket of the percolator and perk until done. Serve hot. Garnish each serving with a lemon slice studded with whole cloves. Yields 1¼ gallons.

Note: For Spiced Iced Tea, fill a glass with ice. Pour tea into the glass until ⅔ full. Fill the remainder of the glass with cold ginger ale.

INDEX

201

Sawdust Pie, Piazza Tea
Room 199
Sweet Potato Pecan Pie, Colony
House 44
Tollhouse Pie, 82 Queen 32

Pie Crusts:
Graham Cracker Crust, Turtle
Deli 107
Quiche Crust, Morris Street Tea
Room 175

ENTREES
Egg Dishes:
Ham and Cheese Omelet,
Capitol 128
Omelette Italiano, California
Dreaming 124
Quiche Angie, Morris Street Tea
Room 175
Scotch Eggs, No. 10 Downing
Street 144

Fowl:
Chicken Kashmir, Up Your
Alley 151
Chicken Pretoria, West Side
Bowery 155
Chicken Reuben,
Farmers Hall 179
Farmhouse Pepper Ducklings,
Willcox Inn 159
Grilled Smoked Quail Stuffed
with Collard Greens,
Carolina's 39
Lemon Basil Chicken,
Bocci's 36
Lemon-Garlic Chicken, Liberty
Hall 184

Low Country Chicken,
Paddock 119
Sautéed Stuffed Chicken in
White Wine, Graystone 167
Suprême de Canette à la Lie du
Vin, Restaurant Million 75
West Indian Chicken Curry,
Noelle's 79

Meat:
Hoppin' John, Middleton
Place 71
Marinated Beef Tenderloin,
Liberty Hall 184
Shepherd's Pie, Tommy
Condon's 96
Veal Marsala, Bonneau's 111
Veal Marsala, Paddock 120
Veal Princess, Up Your
Alley 152

Miscellaneous:
Broccoli Ham Quiche, Turtle
Deli 107
Pasta Rosé, Olive Oil's 148
Pasta with White Clam Sauce,
Villa Tronco 136
Taco Quiche, Newton
House 116

Seafood:
Atlantic Salmon, Captain
Guilds' 27
Carolina Blue Crab and Scallop
Cakes, East Bay Trading
Company 47
Crabmeat à la Poogan's,
Poogan's Porch 84
Flounder Caprice,
Anchorage 100

202